Japanese Hand Guns

Frontispiece: KOMURO MODEL 1905
Very early automatic made by Tomisiro Komuro in Tokyo from 1906 to 1910.
Amount manufactured unknown. Example shown Serial No. 56. Another specimen known with
Serial No. 1172. Caliber 7.65 mm. Excellent workmanship and finish.
Courtesy of Norm Hower

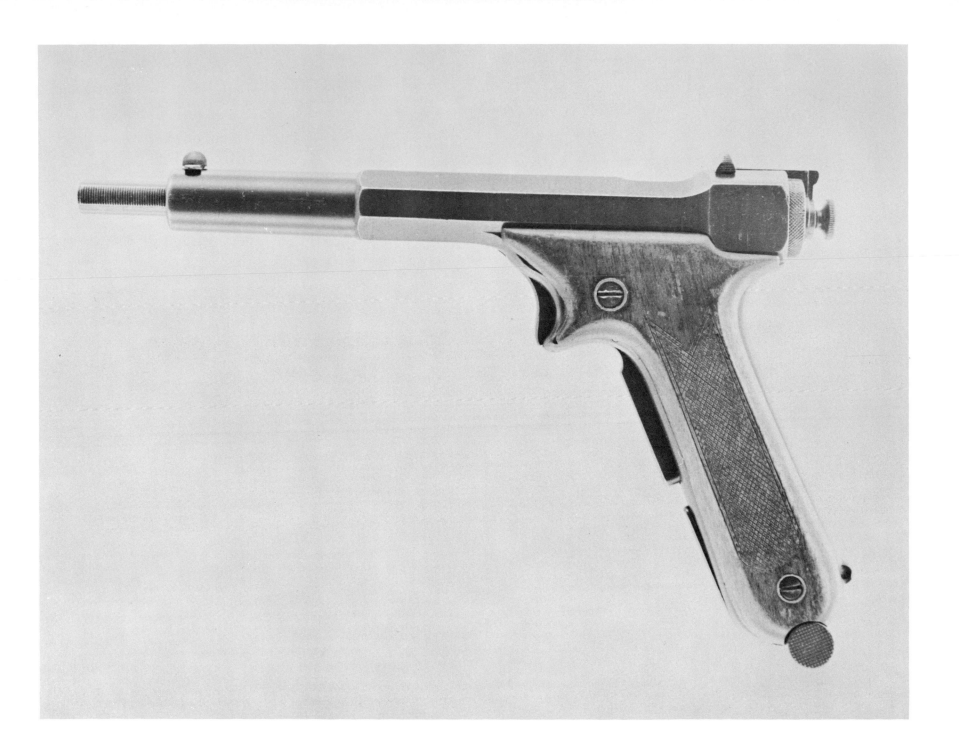

Japanese Hand Guns

by Frederick E. Leithe

BORDEN PUBLISHING COMPANY, ALHAMBRA, CALIFORNIA

Acknowledgments

The successful conclusion of any undertaking can be measured, in part, by the contributions and help of many people. I would like to thank the following for theirs—

Vic Chun—*Started it all*

Arnold Padilla—*Use of his fine drawings*

Larry Baron—*Man responsible for fine photography*

Anne and Harry Jones—*Encouragement and advice*

Patrick Peine, Jr.—*Pictures and statistics*

T. Ohta—*Invaluable accurate information from Japan*

Lee Bishop—*Typing and Editing*

Don Bullock

Bob Butrick

Don Ovall

Wyant La Mont

Norm Hower

Tom Gilbert

Jack Harker

. . . And to the many more collectors, dealers, and friends, whose leads, tips, clues, talk, and patience made this book possible.

All illustrated items unless otherwise noted are from the author's collection.

Introduction

Although this book is intended to be technical rather than historical, a short explanation of markings and models is necessary, as they are closely interconnected with Japanese history.

Japanese Pistols are marked in Japanese, either words or symbols; the latter being used to designate Arsenals. The characters appearing on the right side of the *"Papa"* Nambu Receiver, reading from left to right, are the words *"Nambu Shiki"*, meaning *"Nambu Type"*. On the left side of the Receiver on the Nambu Type 14 (1925) Series, characters read from left to right *"Juyonen Shiki"*, meaning 14 Year Type. On the left side of the Receiver of the Nambu Type 94, characters read from left to right *"Kyuyon Shiki"*, meaning 94 Type. These designations require some explanation.

In Japan, a New Era begins with the enthronement of a new Emperor. The Emperor preceding the present Emperor Hirohito was his father, Taisho. Taisho took the Throne in 1911, so the pistol designation *"Type 14 (1925)"* means the *"Type of the 14th year of the Taisho Reign"* (1911 + 14 = 1925). With the death of Emperor Taisho after 15 years of rule, Emperor Hirohito (Crown Prince during his father's Reign) promptly succeeded to the Throne under the Era Designation of *"Showa"*. Thus such past Era Designations as *"Taisho"* (1912 - 1926), *"Meiji"* (1868 - 1912), *"Keio"* (1865 - 1868), *"Genji"* (1864 - 1865), each indicate the Reigning Period of a particular Emperor.

As the present Emperor Hirohito has Reigned for 42 years since his Enthronement, 1967 is known as the 42nd Year of *"Showa"*. Thus a pistol with the date 10.2 stamped on the frame would denote our year 1935, the second month, February, (1925 + 10 = 1935). The generalized meaning of *"Showa"* is *"Enlightening-Peace"*; the Japanese character-word *"Sho"* meaning *"Enlightenment,"* while *"Wa"* is *"Peace."*

This system of Era Designation goes back 2,625 years to the time that Emperor Jimmu took the Throne as the first Emperor of Japan in 660 B.C.

The Nambu Type 94 (1934) is named according to a different system. From 1926 to 1940 a model was given a number derived from the assumed date of the founding of the Japanese Empire in 660 B.C. The last two digits of the particular year figured on this system were used to designate the model. Since this particular model was adopted in the Japanese Year 2594 (our year 1934), the designation Nambu Type 94 (1934) was assigned as official nomenclature.

Preface

The preparation of this book had as its purpose the desire to identify as many variations of Japanese handguns as possible. I have tried to provide a composite guide for the use of the individual in doing just that.

Relatively little is known about Japanese handguns, and as time pushes their era further back into history, people who do have that information are being inevitably lost. Most, if not all, production records were destroyed by the intensive B-29 incendiary raids. Thus the only ready source of information in Japan now, are the workers who were themselves employed in the arsenals. Simple arithmetic will illustrate the point.

This book is intended to be an identification guide and not a technical or historical work. The information and descriptions are given to the best of my knowledge, and are the result of much research, conversation, and correspondence. I have no doubt that there are many variations, prototypes, and re-work models not shown in this book, and it is my hope that these will be brought forth as its result, for all to see in Volume Two.

Being a collector, the technical terms and names of variations and accessories I have used in this book are those already familiar to collectors. The layman may discover a bit of unfamiliar terminology as a result, but should experience little or no undue difficulty in using the book as it was intended.

Frederick E. Leithe
Malibu, Calif.
1967

Model 26 (1893)
9mm revolver

This pistol was a native Japanese development of the 1890's, although it employs a hinged frame similar to Smith and Wesson, and lockwork and plates similar to Rast & Gasser. It was the official Japanese Non-commissioned Officer's Service Revolver from 1893 to 1904. It continued in service use until 1925, when the Type 14 Nambu Automatic Pistol was officially adopted. It employs a 9mm rimmed center fire cartridge. The bullet is unjacketed lead. Muzzle velocity is approximately 750 feet per second.

Design type: Double action only.
Weight with empty cylinder: 2 pounds.
Overall length: 9.4 inches.
Barrel length: 4.7 inches.
Number of grooves: 4.
Direction of twist: Right.
Cartridge capacity: 6 rounds.

No record is available of when production ceased, but the example on page 21 would indicate that production continued up to 1925. Dismounting procedure follows:
Place muzzle down on a firm surface. Pulling down on the trigger guard will release it from an indention in the frame, permitting it to swing down. The left-hand side plate may then be swung out and readward, exposing all the lockwork. The left stock can now be lifted out, exposing the screws holding the right stock to the frame. Removal of the lockwork is accomplished in the conventional manner. The cylinder is unscrewed from its mounting, and when removed, takes the extractor with it.

MODEL: Model 26 (1893) 9mm Revolver
MANUFACTURER: Prototype — Koishigawa Arsenal.
SIGHTS: Pinned Front, Grooved Rear.
GRIPS: Finely checkered walnut.
SAFETY: None.
DESIGNATION: Prototype—used for testing and evaluation.

MARKINGS

CHAMBER: None.
FRAME: None.
RECEIVER: None.
DISTINCTIVE FEATURES: Excellent finish and workmanship. Slightly differently shaped hammer. Serial No. 3 appears on all parts internally.

MODEL:	Model 26 (1893) 9mm Revolver
MANUFACTURER:	Koishigawa, Tokyo, Japan. Later to become Kokura Arsenal.
SIGHTS:	Pinned Front, Grooved Rear.
GRIPS:	Light walnut with medium checkering.
SAFETY:	None.
DESIGNATION:	Japanese Service Revolver from 1893 to 1904.

MARKINGS

CHAMBER:	None.
FRAME:	Arsenal Mark, Model Identification, Serial Number.
RECEIVER:	None.
DISTINCTIVE FEATURES:	Standard production version. Very good finish and workmanship.

MODEL: Model 26 (1893) 9mm Revolver
MANUFACTURER: Koishigawa, Tokyo, Japan. Later to become Kokura Arsenal.
SIGHTS: Pinned Front, Grooved Rear.
GRIPS: Mahogany with horizontal serrations.
SAFETY: None.
DESIGNATION: Japanese Service Revolver from 1893 to 1904

MARKINGS

CHAMBER: None.
FRAME: Arsenal Mark, Model Identification, Serial Number.
RECEIVER: None.
DISTINCTIVE FEATURES: Crude grips and somewhat rougher finish indicate this to be of later manufacture; possibly later than 1925.

These specifications and dismounting procedures will cover both early and late type *"Papa"* Nambus, originally developed by Colonel Kijiro Nambu in 1904. The caliber is 8mm; the cartridge bottlenecked and rimless. The bullet is full-jacketed, weighing 102 grains. Muzzle velocity is 950 feet per second. This same cartridge is used in all 8mm Japanese pistols.

The Nambu 1904
8mm pistol

Design Type: Recoil operated, locked bolt.

Weight with empty magazine: 1 pound, 15 ounces.

Overall length: 9 inches.

Barrel length: 4.7 inches to Bolt Face.

Number of Grooves: 6.

Direction of twist: Right.

Magazine capacity: 8 rounds.

Magazine weight loaded: 6.3 ounces.

Some variations of this model were manufactured to accept a shoulder stock holster. This slipped into a groove on rear of frame much like the Mauser. The holster was leather covered wood with a telescoping bottom extension to convert it to a shoulder stock. Dismounting procedure is as follows:

Remove the magazine. Push the muzzle against a solid object, and while the barrel is back about a quarter of an inch, depress the magazine catch at the same time that you pull the trigger guard down. This assembly may then be moved. Again pushing the barrel back and holding it, give the cocking piece lock a quarter turn and remove it. The striker and spring will then come out. The barrel and breechblock assembly may then be slid forward out of the receiver. The breechblock and recoil spring may then be withdrawn.

Parts Breakdown

"PAPA"

1. Frame
2. Barrel & Receiver
3. Locking Block
4. Bolt
5. Extractor
6. Firing Pin
7. Tangent Sight
8. Range Selector
9. Lock Spring
10. Range Selector Lock
11. Sight Spring
12. Cocking Piece
13. Firing Pin Spring
14. Bolt Lock & Firing Pin Spring Guide
15. Locking Block Spring
16. Sear Bar
17. Sear Spring
18. Sear Bar Plunger Spring
19. Scar Bar Plunger
20. Sear Bar Plunger Holding Pin
21. Sear Pivot Pin
22. Magazine Release Body
23. Magazine Release Button
24. Magazine Release Button Spring
25. Recoil Spring
26. Recoil Spring Guide
27. Grip Stock — Left shown
28. Grip Stock
29. Grip Screw
30. Grip Screw
31. Safety Spring
32. Safety
33. Trigger
34. Safety Pivot Pin
35. Trigger Guard
36. Trigger Pivot Pin
37. Magazine Follower
38. Magazine Spring
39. Loading Button
40. Magazine Body
41. Base Pin — Rear
42. Base Pin — Front
43. Magazine Base

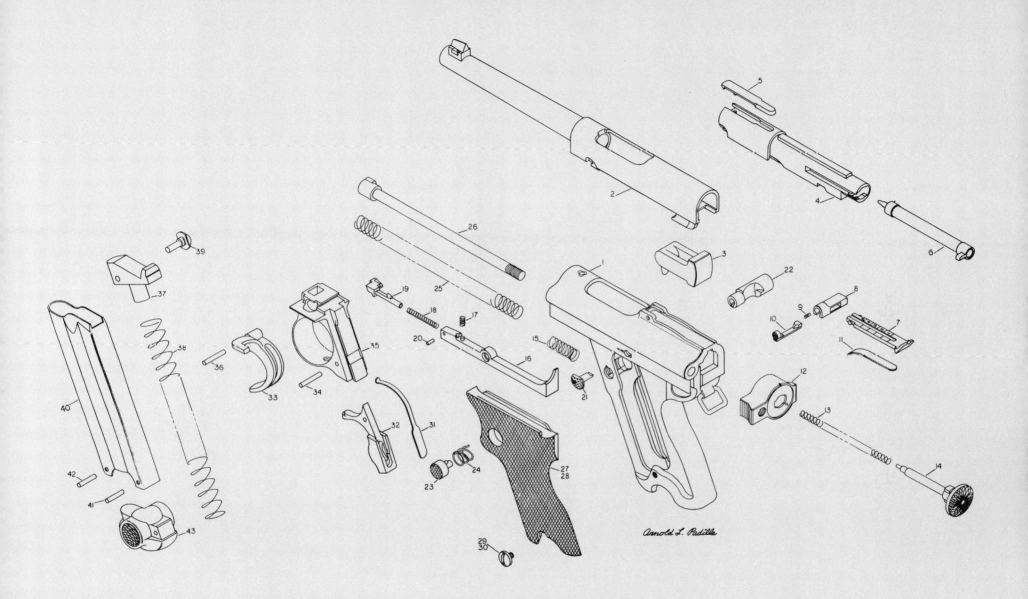

Arnold L. Padilla

MODEL: Nambu 1904 8mm Pistol
MANUFACTURER: Kayoba Factory Ltd., Tokyo, Japan.
SIGHTS: Dovetailed Front, Radial Leaf Rear, graduated in 100 meters from 100 to 500 meters.
GRIPS: Checkered walnut.
SAFETY: Grip Safety, located on front of grip frame.
DESIGNATION: Commercial; distribution through Imperial Sales Agency and unofficial Japanese Army use.

MARKINGS

CHAMBER: Commercial Marking.
FRAME: None.
RECEIVER: Model Identification and Serial Number on right side only.
DISTINCTIVE FEATURES: Very small trigger guard, wooden bottom Magazine, rear of frame slotted for stock, rounded trigger. Excellent blued finish and workmanship throughout. Trigger, Extractor, Magazine Release Button, and Bolt Locking Retainer are straw colored. Commonly referred to as "Peanut Guard Nambu".

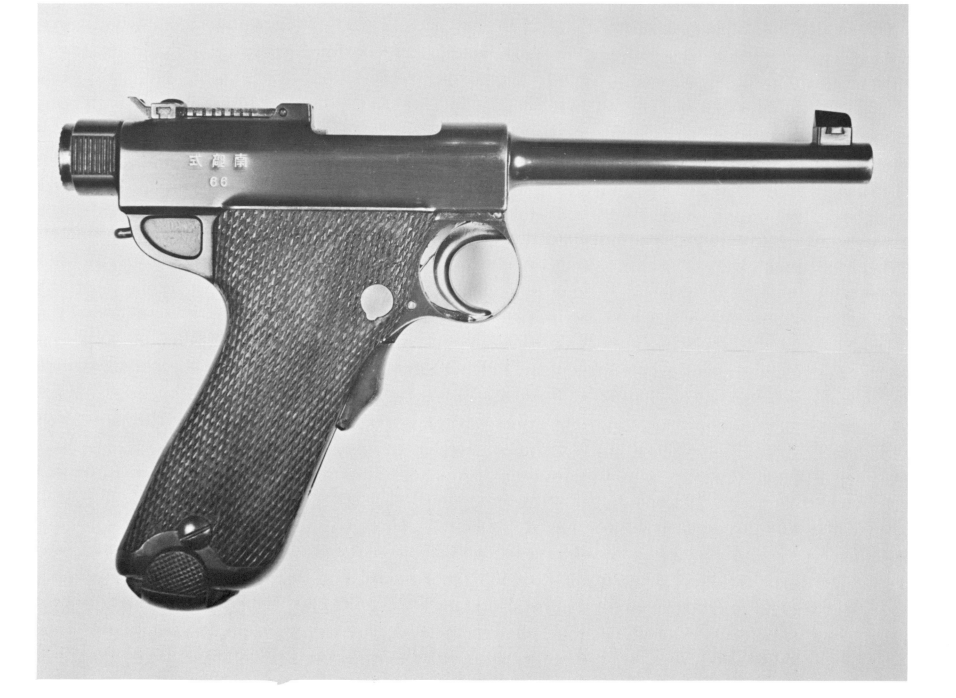

MODEL:	Nambu 1904 8mm Pistol (Early Type)
MANUFACTURER:	Tokyo Arsenal.
SIGHTS:	Dovetailed Front, Radial Leaf Rear, graduated in 100 meters, from 100 to 500 meters.
GRIPS:	Checkered Walnut.
SAFETY:	Grip Safety, located on front of grip frame.
DESIGNATION:	Commercial Sales Model, for officers of Japanese Armed Forces.

MARKINGS

CHAMBER:	Arsenal Mark.
FRAME:	None.
RECEIVER:	On left side, Characters for *"Army Type"*. On right side, Characters for *"Nambu Type"*, and Serial Number.
DISTINCTIVE FEATURES:	Later production of 1904. Modifications include larger Trigger Guard, Aluminum Bottom Magazine, improved Grips, Square Side Trigger, and Cocking Piece concave instead of convex in area of serrations. The blued finish is excellent with the Trigger, Extractor, Magazine Release Button, and Bolt Locking Retainer straw colored. Commonly known as *"Papa Nambu"*

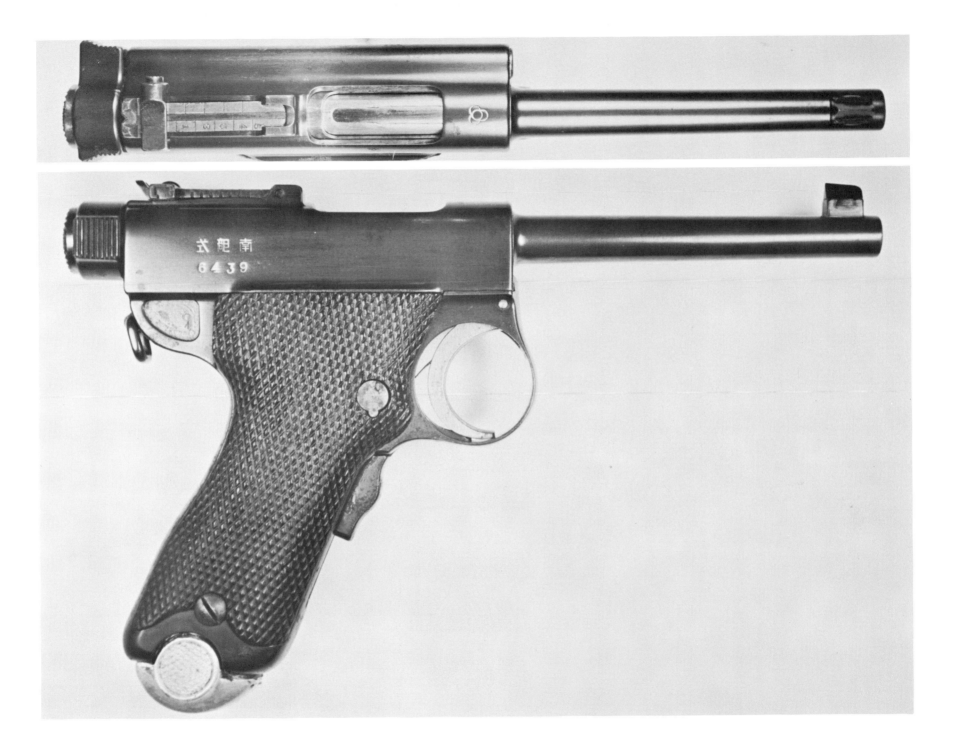

MODEL: Nambu 1904 8mm Pistol (Early Type)
MANUFACTURER: Tokyo Arsenal and Tokyo Gas and Electric.
SIGHTS: Dovetailed Front, Radial Leaf Rear, graduated in 100 meters. from 100 to 500 meters.
GRIPS: Checkered Walnut.
SAFETY: Grip Safety, located on front of Grip Frame.
DESIGNATION: Commercial Sales Model, for Officers of Japanese Armed Forces and Export Trade.

MARKINGS

CHAMBER: T.G.E. enclosed in circle.
FRAME: None.
RECEIVER: On left side, Characters for *"Army Type."*
On right side, Characters for *"Nambu Type,"* Serial Number, and Tokyo Arsenal Symbol.
DISTINCTIVE FEATURES: Arsenal Symbol on side denotes arsenal re-work. Possibily turned in for re-building and re-finishing. Retains all modifications of later Production Model. The blued finish is excellent with the Trigger, Extractor, Magazine Release Button, and Bolt Locking Retainer straw colored. Commonly known as "Tokyo Re-work."

MODEL: Nambu 1904 8mm Pistol (Later Type)
MANUFACTURER: Tokyo Gas and Electric Company.
SIGHTS: Dovetailed Front, Radial Leaf Rear, graduated in 100 meters, from 100 to 500 meters.
GRIPS: Checkered Walnut.
SAFETY: Grip Safety, located on front of Grip Frame.
DESIGNATION: Commercial Sales Model, for Officers of Japanese Armed Forces.

MARKINGS

CHAMBER: T.G.E. enclosed in a circle.
FRAME: None.
RECEIVER: On Left Side, Characters for *"Army Type."*
On Right Side, Characters for *"Nambu Type,"*
Serial Number, and Naval Anchor Stamp.
DISTINCTIVE FEATURES: Anchor stamped on right side near Serial Number shows this example was owned by a Naval Officer. Low Serial Number denotes early production of version with Stock Slot on Rear of Frame and solid area on sides of Frame near top rear of Grips. Stamped Anchor Re-works will always have Stock Slot filled by Arsenal during re-work as Navy deemed open slot dangerous to the hand. Retains all modifications of later Production Model. The blued finish is excellent with the Trigger, Extractor, Magazine Release Button, and Bolt Locking Retainer straw colored. Commonly known as "Naval Re-work."

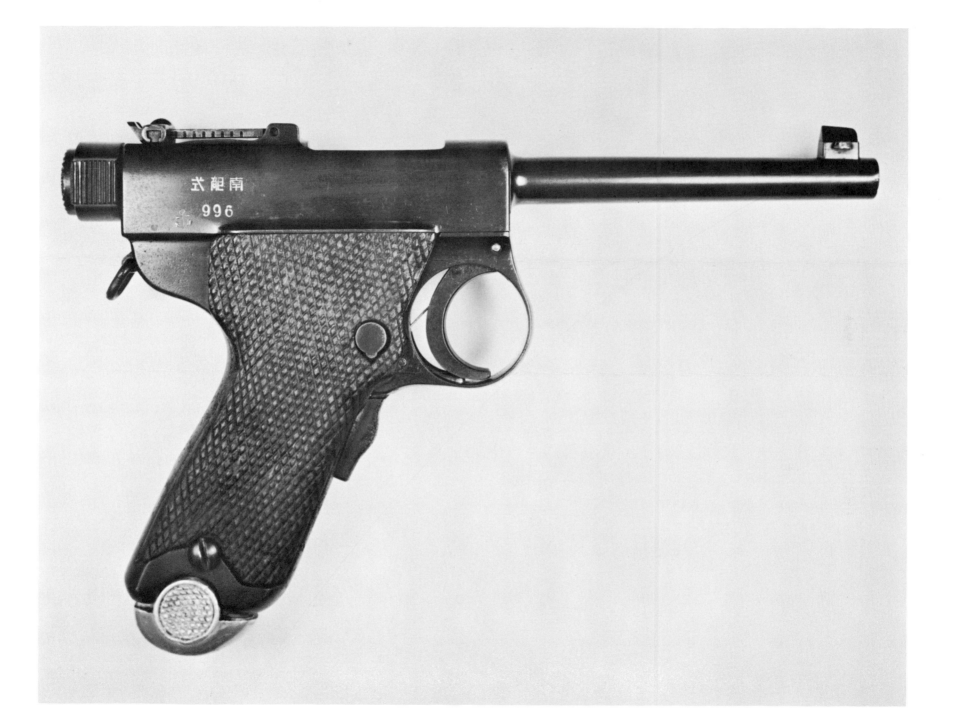

MODEL:	Nambu 1904 8mm Pistol (Later Type)
MANUFACTURER:	Tokyo Gas and Electric Company.
SIGHTS:	Dovetailed Front, Radial Leaf Rear, graduated in 100 meters, from 100 to 500 meters.
GRIPS:	Checkered Walnut.
SAFETY:	Grip Safety, located on front of Grip Frame.
DESIGNATION:	Commercial Sales Model, for Officers of Japanese Armed Forces, and in this case specifically, a Japanese Naval Officer.

MARKINGS

CHAMBER:	T.G.E. enclosed in a circle.
FRAME:	None.
RECEIVER:	On Left Side, Characters for *"Army Type."* On Right Side, Characters for *"Nambu Type,"* Serial Number and engraved Naval Anchor.
DISTINCTIVE FEATURES:	On this variation the Anchor is engraved, not stamped, which indicates the weapon was specifically contracted for in production. Retains Solid Frame, but has no Stock Slot. Retains all modifications of later production model. The blued finish is excellent with the Trigger, Extractor, Magazine Release Button, and Bolt Locking Retainer straw colored. Commonly known as a *"Naval Contract."*

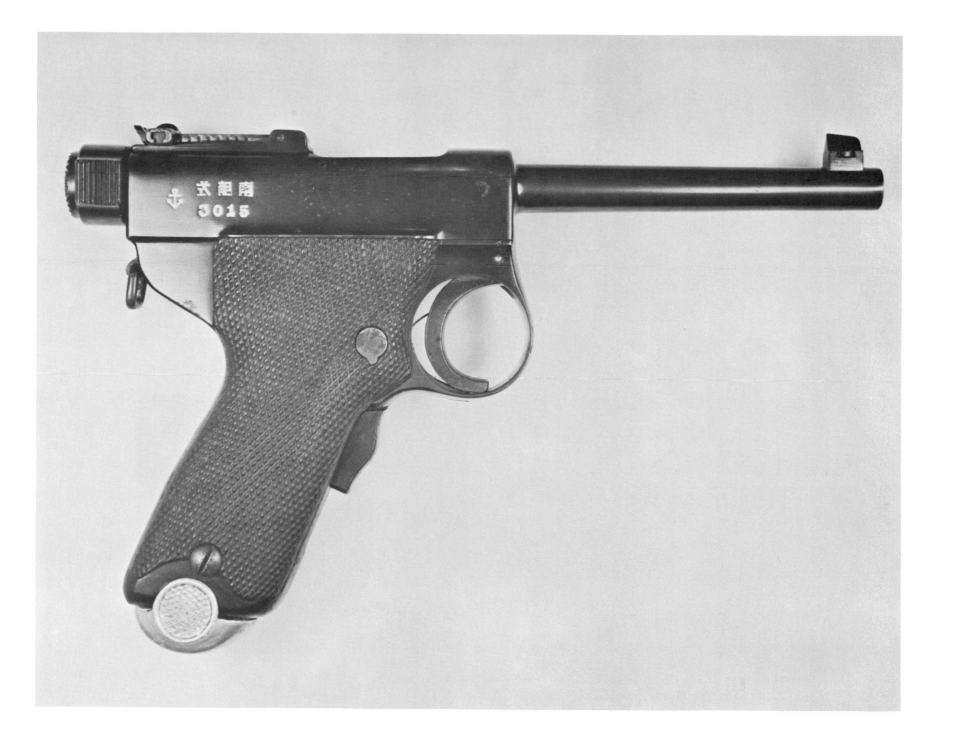

式艦南
3015

Nambu type pistol
"Baby Nambu"

Of all Japanese Pistols, this one is the most desirable, and at the same time the least known, insofar as facts and figures are concerned. The design and operation are identical to those of the Nambu 1904 8mm Pistol in all respects; it has been encountered with the same manufacturing marks as the *"Papa"*, so it would seem logical to assume that development and production of the two pistols occurred at the same time. The small caliber and overall size made this pistol strictly a close personal defense weapon. The very existence of the pistol, as reported by General Hatcher in 1935, was doubted and in some quarters openly laughed at, until actual examples were encountered late in World War II. The pistol employs a 7mm Nambu bottleneck center fire cartridge. The bullet is full-jacketed, weighing 56 grains. Muzzle velocity is approximately 800 feet per second.

Design type: Recoil operated, locked bolt.
Weight with empty magazine: 1 pound, 7 ounces.
Overall length: 6.75 inches.
Barrel length: 3.25 inches.
Number of Grooves: 6.
Direction of twist: Right.
Magazine capacity: 7 rounds.

The fine finish and workmanship throughout indicate this particular model was intended for a very select group of customers. The high esteem in which this pistol was held is demonstrated by the fact that the Emperor selected it as his presentation pistol. Dismounting procedure is the same as that for the 1904 Model *"Papa"* Nambu.

Parts List

"BABY" NAMBU

1. Frame
2. Recoil Spring
3. Recoil Spring Guide
4. Cocking Piece
5. Firing Pin Spring
6. Bolt Lock and Firing Pin Spring Guide
7. Locking Block
8. Firing Pin
9. Bolt
10. Extractor
11. Barrel & Receiver
12. Magazine Release Body
13. Magazine Release Button Spring
14. Magazine Release Button
15. Locking Block Spring
16. Sear Bar
17. Sear Spring
18. Sear Bar Plunger Spring
19. Sear Bar Plunger
20. Sear Bar Plunger Holding Pin
21. Sear Pivot Pin
22. Trigger Guard
23. Trigger
24. Trigger Pivot Pin
25. Safety
26. Safety Spring
27. Safety Pivot Pin
28. Grip Stock—Left shown
29. Grip Stock
30. Grip Screw
31. Grip Screw
32. Magazine Body
33. Magazine Spring
34. Magazine Follower
35. Loading Button
36. Magazine Base
37. Base Pin—Front
38. Base Pin—Rear

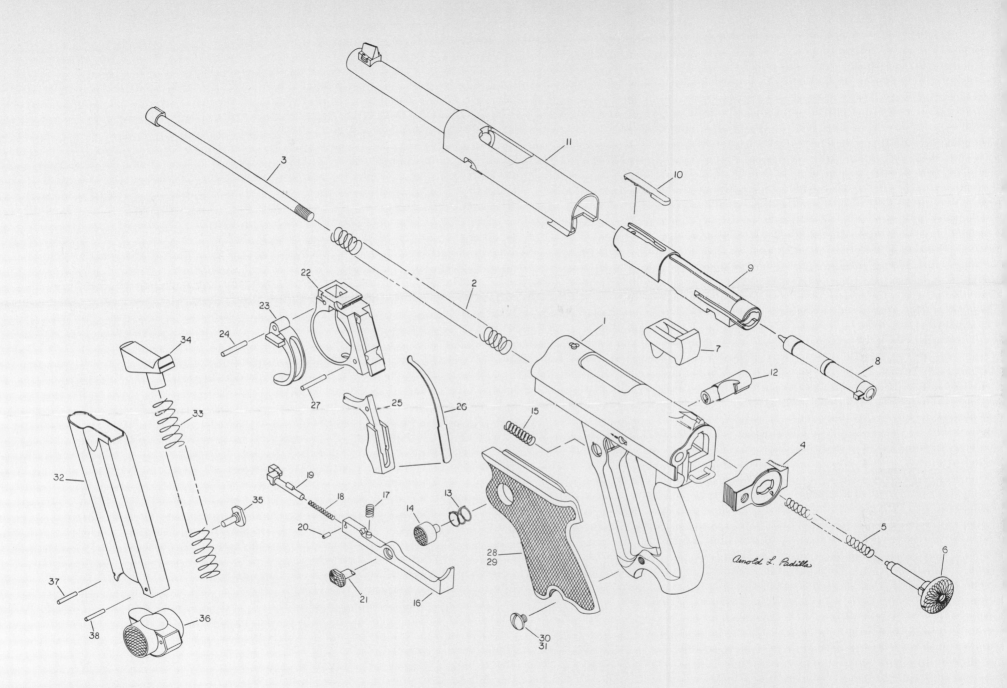

Arnold L. Padilla

MODEL:	Nambu Type Pistol *("Baby Nambu")*
MANUFACTURER:	Tokyo Gas and Electric Company, Toyko, Japan.
SIGHTS:	Dovetail Front, "V" Notch Rear.
GRIPS:	Checkered walnut.
SAFETY:	Grip safety located on front of grip frame.
DESIGNATION:	Commercial; Original commercial sales production.

MARKINGS

CHAMBER:	Commercial Marking.
FRAME:	None.
RECEIVER:	Serial Number and Model Identification on right side.
DISTINCTIVE FEATURES:	Produced by hand production methods. All examples of this model finely finished with excellent workmanship throughout.

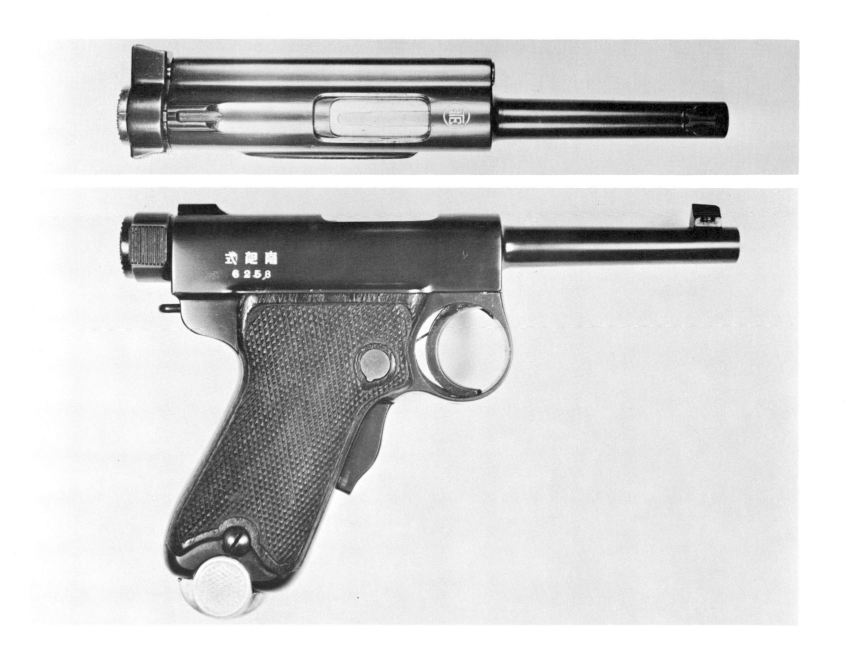

MODEL: Nambu Type Pistol *("Baby Nambu")*
MANUFACTURER: Kayoba Factory, Tokyo. Later taken over by Kokura Arsenal.
SIGHTS: Dovetailed Front, "V" Notched Rear.
GRIPS: Checkered Walnut.
SAFETY: Grip Safety located on front of grip frame.
DESIGNATION: Production Model. Purchased by Officers in all branches of service as side arm.

MARKINGS

CHAMBER: Arsenal Marking.
FRAME: None.
RECEIVER: Serial Number and Model Identification on right side.
DISTINCTIVE FEATURES: Produced by hand production methods. All examples of this model finely finished with excellent workmanship throughout.

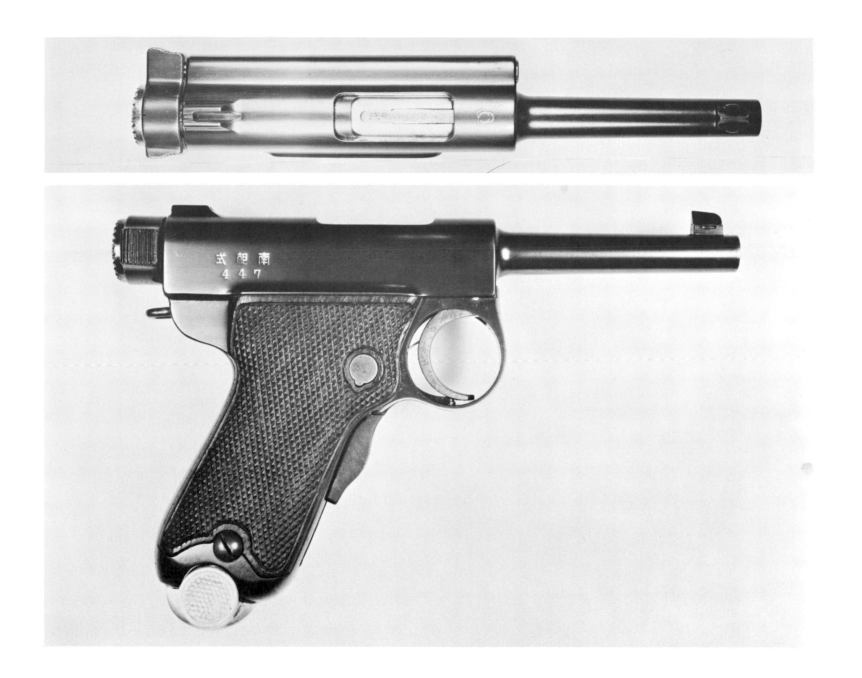

MODEL: Nambu Type Pistol *("Baby Nambu")*
MANUFACTURER: Kayoba Factory, Tokyo. Later taken over by Kokura Arsenal.
SIGHTS: Dovetailed Front, "V" Notched Rear.
GRIPS: Checkered walnut.
SAFETY: Grip Safety, located on front of grip frame.
DESIGNATION: Presentation Model.

MARKINGS

CHAMBER: Arsenal Marking.
FRAME: None.
RECEIVER: Serial Number and Model Identification on right side. Engraved Characters in front of rear sight on top.
DISTINCTIVE FEATURES: Characters on top of receiver identify this example as Emperor's Presentation Model, translate to read "Imperial gift in honor of personal achievements". Only students graduating from certain Military Service Schools with top honors received this distinction. It is estimated that less than 100 were presented. A very rare variation seldom encountered by collectors.

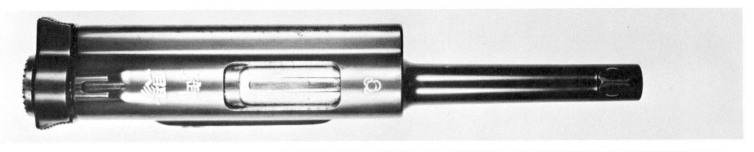

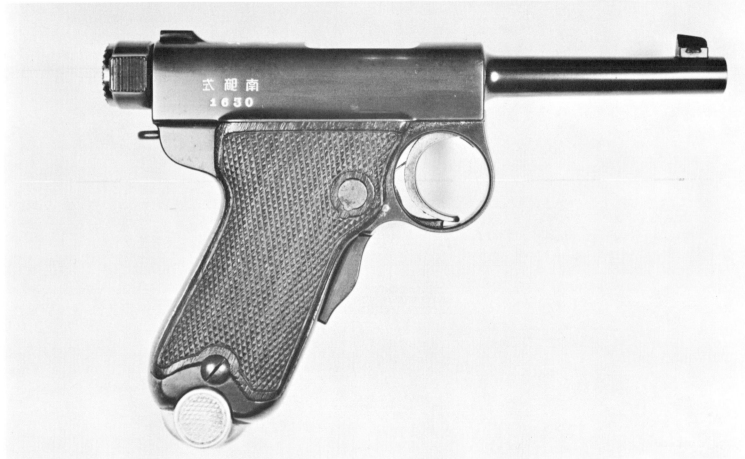

MODEL: Nambu Type Pistol *("Baby Nambu")*
MANUFACTURER: Kayoba Factory, Tokyo. Later taken over by Kokura Arsenal.
SIGHTS: Dovetailed Front, "V" Notch Rear.
GRIPS: Checkered Walnut.
SAFETY: Grip Safety located at front of Grip Frame.
DESIGNATION: Prototype — used for testing and evaluation.

MARKINGS

CHAMBER: Arsenal Marking.
FRAME: None.
RECEIVER: Model identification on right side.
DISTINCTIVE FEATURES: No Serial Numbers appear on outside of gun. All parts serialized internally. Evidently done to enhance appearance when shown to prospective customers or Evaluation Boards. Exceptional finish and fine fitting of working parts.

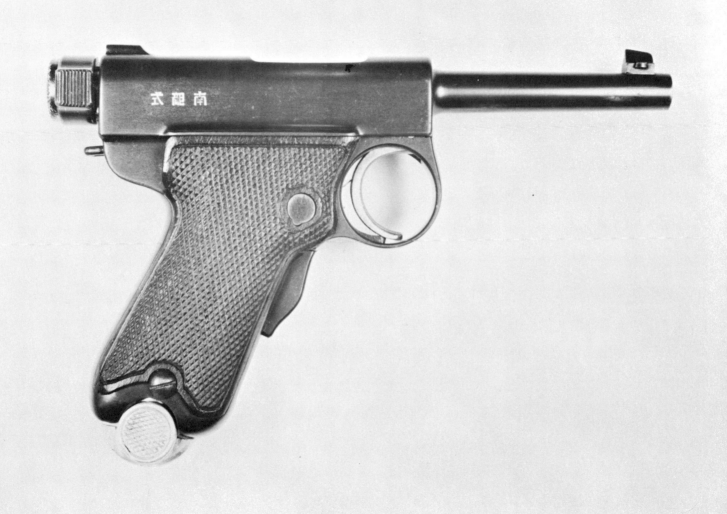

This model replaced Model 1904 Pistol and Model 26 Revolver in Armed Forces use. Production from 1925 until the end of the war made this the most often encountered wartime pistol. Two basic models were produced, with the elongated trigger guard adopted in 1939 to facilitate firing with gloves on. This was the result of experience from campaigns in Northern China and Manchuria.

Type 14 year (1925) 8mm pistol

Design type: Recoil operated, locked bolt.
Weight with empty magazine: 2 pounds.
Overall length: 9 inches.
Barrel length: 4.7 inches to face of bolt (recessed)
Number of grooves: 6.
Direction of twist: Right.
Magazine capacity: 8 rounds.
Magazine weight loaded: 6.3 ounces.

This is a simple, well designed pistol. Very few moving parts and light recoil make it a pleasant weapon to fire. Dismounting procedure is as follows:

Push in the head of the firing pin spring guide which protrudes through the center of the cocking piece and turn the cocking piece. As the piece is removed the spring will force the extension out of its seat in the bolt. The pin and its spring may now be taken out. With magazine removed, press muzzle on a solid surface to push the barrel back at the same time that the magazine catch is pushed in. The left-hand stock should be removed to facilitate sliding the trigger guard assembly out. The barrel assembly may now be slid forward on its grooves out of the receiver. The locking bolt may be taken off its pivot on the barrel extension. This block must be replaced before firing the weapon. The pistol can be assembled without it, and lack of the block makes this a blowback pistol, and the cartridge is powerful enough to damage an unlocked action. The breechblock and the recoil springs may now be removed from the barrel extension.

Parts List

MODEL 14

1. Frame
2. Sear Spring
3. Magazine Release Spring
4. Sear Pivot Pin
5. Sear Bar
6. Magazine Release Catch
7. Safety Lever
8. Barrel & Receiver
9. Locking Block
10. Bolt
11. Extractor
12. Recoil Spring
13. Recoil Spring
14. Firing Pin — Early Type shown
15. Firing Pin Spring
16. Firing Pin Spring Guide and Bolt Nut Lock
17. Bolt Nut — Cocking Piece Early Style
17A. Bolt Nut — Cocking Piece Late Style
18. Magazine Safety Block
19. Magazine Safety Spring Guide
20. Magazine Safely Spring
21. Magazine Safety Pivot Pin
22. Locking Block Spring
23. Grip Stock — Left shown
24. Grip Stock
25. Grip Screw
26. Grip Screw
27. Trigger Guard — Early Style
28. Trigger Guard — Late Style
29. Magazine Body
30. Magazine Follower
31. Loading Button
32. Magazine Spring
33. Magazine Base
34. Base Pin — Front
35. Base Pin — Rear

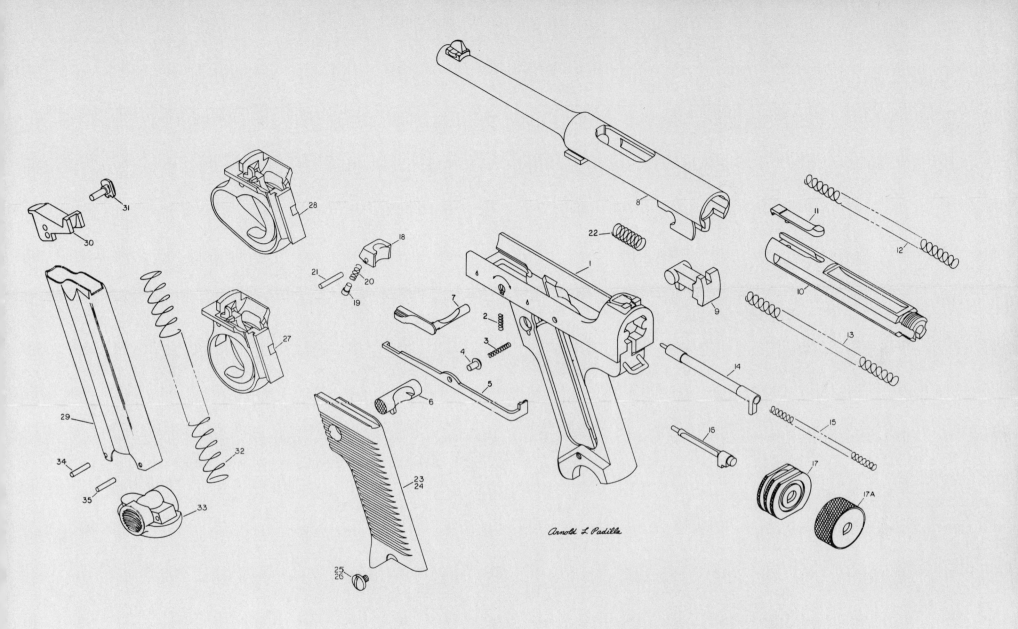

Arnold L. Padilla

MODEL:	Type 14 Year (1925)
MANUFACTURER:	Nagoya Arsenal.
SIGHTS:	Front — Dovetail Blade.
	Rear — Undercut Notch.
GRIPS:	Serrated light-colored Walnut.
SAFETY:	Manual Thumb — Left Side.
DESIGNATION:	Japanese Armed Forces Model, primarily Army, but has appeared with Naval markings.

MARKINGS

CHAMBER:	None.
FRAME:	Year and month of manufacture (1927 - July), Nagoya Arsenal Symbol, Character for *"Showa."*
RECEIVER:	Serial Number on right side, Model Designation (14 Year Type), and *"Safe"* and *"Fire"* Characters for Safety Lever on left side.
DISTINCTIVE FEATURES:	Very low Serial Number. Fine blued finish and workmanship. Aluminum Bottom nickel-plated Magazine. Safety Lever, Trigger, Sear Bar, and Magazine Release Button straw colored.

MODEL: Type 14 Year (1925)

MANUFACTURER: Kokura Arsenal.

SIGHTS: Front — Dove Tail Blade.
Rear — Undercut Notch.

GRIPS: Serrated light-colored Walnut.

SAFETY: Manual Thumb — Left Side.

DESIGNATION: Japanese Armed Forces Model, primarily Army, but has appeared with Naval markings.

MARKINGS

CHAMBER: None.

FRAME: Year and month of manufacture (1928 — March), Character for *"Showa."*

RECEIVER: Serial Number and Kokura Arsenal Symbol on right side. Model Designation (14 Year Type), and *"Safe"* and *"Fire"* Characters for Safety Lever on left side.

DISTINCTIVE FEATURES: Low Serial Number. Fine blued finish and workmanship. Aluminum Bottom nickel-plated Magazine. Safety Lever, Trigger, Sear Bar, and Magazine Release Button straw colored.

MODEL:	Type 14 Year (1925)
MANUFACTURER:	Kokura Arsenal.
SIGHTS:	Front — Dove Tail Blade.
	Rear — Undercut Notch.
GRIPS:	Serrated light-colored Walnut.
SAFETY:	Manual Thumb — Left side.
DESIGNATION:	Japanese Armed Forces Model, primarily Army, but has appeared with Naval markings.

MARKINGS

CHAMBER:	None.
FRAME:	Year and Month of manufacture (1929 - February), and Character for *"Showa."*
RECEIVER:	Serial Number and Kokura Arsenal Symbol on right side. Model Designation (14 Year Type) and *"Safe"* and *"Fire"* Characters for Safety Lever on left side.
DISTINCTIVE FEATURES:	Four digit Serial Number. Fine blued finish and workmanship. Aluminum Bottom nickel-plated Magazine. Safety Lever, Trigger, Sear Bar, and Magazine Release Button straw colored.

MODEL: Type 14 Year (1925)

MANUFACTURER: Kokura Arsenal.

SIGHTS: Front — Dove Tail Blade.

Rear — Undercut Notch.

GRIPS: Serrated light-colored Walnut.

SAFETY: Manual Thumb — Left side.

DESIGNATION: Japanese Armed Forces Model, primarily Army, but has appeared with Naval markings.

MARKINGS

CHAMBER: None.

FRAME: Year and Month of manufacture (1930 - December), Character for *"Showa"* and inspection stamp.

RECEIVER: Serial Number and Kokura Arsenal Symbol on right side. Model Designation (14 Year Type) and *"Safe"* and *"Fire"* Characters for Safety Lever on left side.

DISTINCTIVE FEATURES: Fine blued finish and workmanship. Aluminum Bottom nickel-plated Magazine. Safety Lever, Trigger, Sear Bar, and Magazine Release Button straw colored.

MODEL: Type 14 Year (1925)

MANUFACTURER: Kokura Arsenal.

SIGHTS: Front — Dove Tail Blade.

Rear — Undercut Notch.

GRIPS: Serrated light-colored Walnut.

SAFETY: Manual Thumb — Left side.

DESIGNATION: Japanese Armed Forces Model, primarily Army, but has appeared with Naval markings.

MARKINGS

CHAMBER: None.

FRAME: Year and Month of Manufacture (1931 - January), Character for *"Showa,"* and inspection stamp.

RECEIVER: Serial Number and Kokura Arsenal Symbol on right side. Model Designation (14 Year Type) and *"Safe"* and *"Fire"* Characters for Safety Lever on left side.

DISTINCTIVE FEATURES: Fine blued finish and workmanship. Aluminum Bottom nickel-plated Magazine. Safety Lever, Trigger, Sear Bar and Magazine Release Button straw colored.

MODEL:	Type 14 Year (1925)
MANUFACTURER:	Nagoya Arsenal.
SIGHTS:	Front — Dove Tail Blade.
	Rear — Undercut Notch.
GRIPS:	Serrated Mahogany.
SAFETY:	Manual Thumb — Left side.
DESIGNATION:	Japanese Armed Forces Model, primarily Army, but has appeared with Naval markings.

MARKINGS

CHAMBER:	None.
FRAME:	Year and Month of Manufacture (1932 - July), Character for *"Showa,"* and inspection stamps.
RECEIVER:	Serial Number and Nagoya Arsenal Symbol on right side. Model Designation (14 Year Type) and *"Safe"* and *"Fire"* Characters for Safety Lever on left side.
DISTINCTIVE FEATURES:	Fine blued finish and workmanship. Aluminum Bottom nickel-plated Magazine. Safety Lever, Trigger, Sear Bar, and Magazine Release Button straw colored.

MODEL:	Type 14 Year (1925)
MANUFACTURER:	Kokura Arsenal.
SIGHTS:	Front — Dove Tail Blade.
	Rear — Undercut Notch.
GRIPS:	Serrated Mahogany.
SAFETY:	Manual Thumb — Left side.
DESIGNATION:	Japanese Armed Forces Model, Primarily Army, but has appeared with Naval markings.

MARKINGS

CHAMBER:	None.
FRAME:	Year and Month of Manufacture (1933 - February), Character for *"Showa,"* and inspection stamp.
RECEIVER:	Serial Number and Kokura Arsenal Symbol on right side. Model Designation (14 Year Type), and *"Safe"* and *"Fire"* Characters for Safety Lever on left side.
DISTINCTIVE FEATURES:	Fine blued finish and workmanship. Aluminum Bottom nickel-plated Magazine. Safety Lever, Trigger, Sear Bar, and Magazine Release Button straw colored.

MODEL: Type 14 Year (1925)
MANUFACTURER: Nagoya Army Ordnance; Nambu Factory.
SIGHTS: Front — Dove Tail Blade.
Rear — Undercut Notch.
GRIPS: Serrated Mahogany.
SAFETY: Manual Thumb — Left side.
DESIGNATION: Japanese Armed Forces Model, primarily Army, but has appeared with Naval markings.

MARKINGS

CHAMBER: None.
FRAME: Year and Month of manufacture (1934 - January), Character for *"Showa,"* and inspection stamp.
RECEIVER: Serial Number and Nagoya Arsenal Symbol with first Character of name *"Nambu."*
DISTINCTIVE FEATURES: Fine blued finish and workmanship. Aluminum Bottom nickel-plated Magazine. Safety Lever, Trigger, Sear Bar, and Magazine Release Button straw colored.

MODEL: Type 14 Years.

MANUFACTURER: Nagoya Army Ordnance; Nambu Factory.

SIGHTS: Front — Dove Tail Blade.

Rear — Undercut Notch.

GRIPS: Serrated Mahogany.

SAFETY: Manual Thumb — Left side.

DESIGNATION: Japanese Armed Forces Model, primarily Army, but has appeared with Naval markings.

MARKINGS

CHAMBER: None.

FRAME: Year and Month of manufacture (1935 - February), Character for *"Showa,"* and inspection stamp.

RECEIVER: Serial Number and Nagoya Arsenal Symbol with first Character of name *"Nambu."*

DISTINCTIVE FEATURES: Fine blued finish and workmanship. Aluminum Bottom nickel-plated Magazine. Safety Lever, Trigger, Sear Bar, and Magazine Release Button straw colored.

MODEL:	Type 14 Year (1925)
MANUFACTURER:	Nagoya Army Ordnance; Nambu Factory.
SIGHTS:	Front — Dove Tail Blade.
	Rear — Undercut Notch.
GRIPS:	Serrated Mahogany.
SAFETY:	Manual Thumb — Left side.
DESIGNATION:	Japanese Armed Forces Model, primarily Army, but has appeared with Naval markings.

MARKINGS

CHAMBER:	None.
FRAME:	Year and Month of manufacture (1936 - March), Character for *"Showa,"* and inspection stamps.
RECEIVER:	Serial Number and Nagoya Arsenal Symbol with first Character of name *"Nambu."*
DISTINCTIVE FEATURES:	Fine blued finish and workmanship. Aluminum Bottom nickel-plated Magazine. Safety Lever, Trigger, Sear Bar, and Magazine Release Button straw colored.

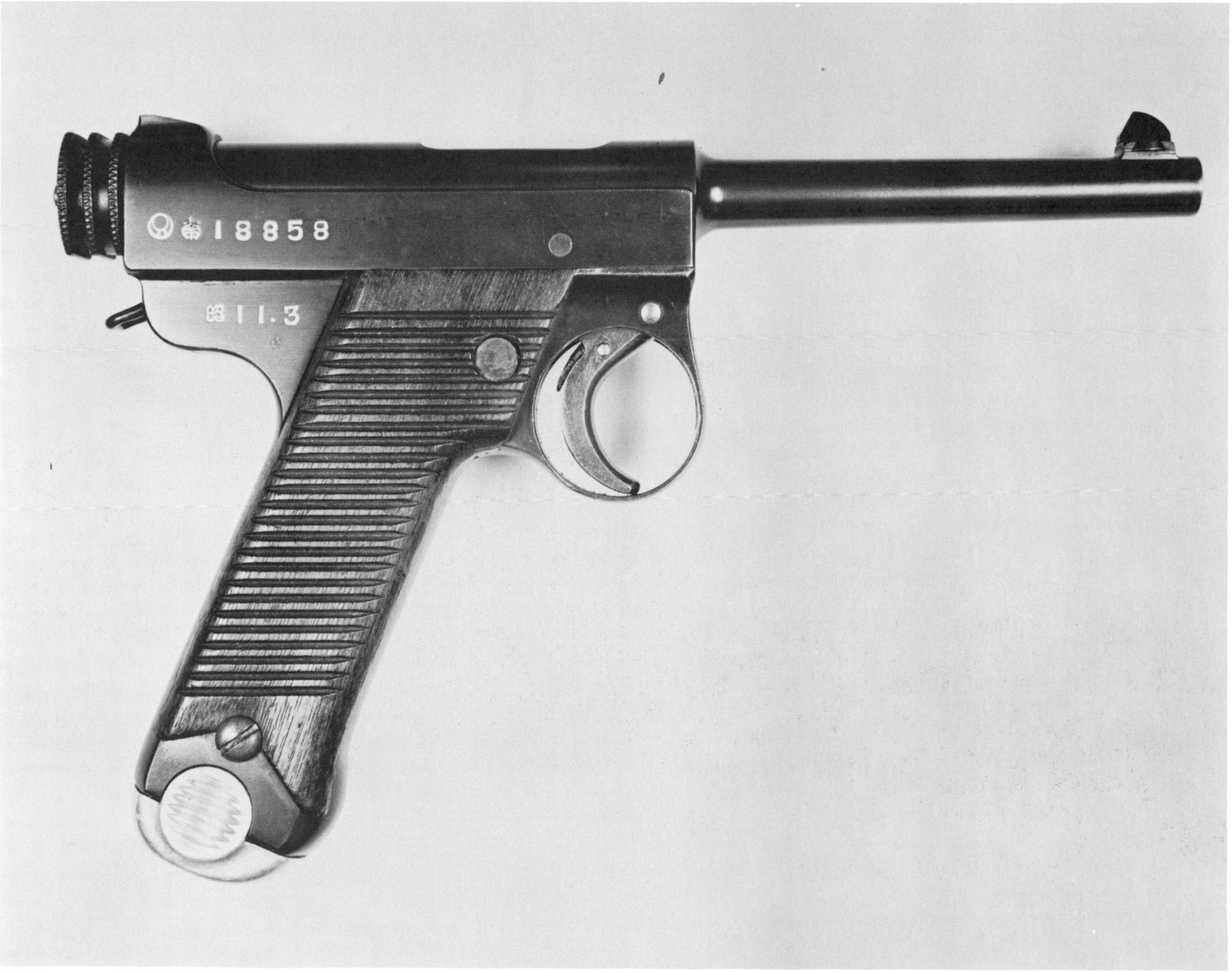
18858
昭11.3

MODEL: Type 14 Year (1925)

MANUFACTURER: Nagoya Army Ordnance; Nambu Factory.

SIGHTS: Front — Dove Tail Blade.

Rear — Undercut Notch.

GRIPS: Serrated Mahogany.

SAFETY: Manual Thumb — Left side.

DESIGNATION: Japanese Armed Forces Model, primarily Army, but has appeared with Naval markings.

MARKINGS

CHAMBER: None.

FRAME: Year and Month of manufacture (1937 - March), Character for *"Showa,"* and inspection stamp.

RECEIVER: Serial Number and Nagoya Arsenal Symbol with first Character of name *"Nambu."*

DISTINCTIVE FEATURES: Fine blued finish and workmanship. Aluminum Bottom nickel-plated Magazine. Safety Lever, Trigger, Sear Bar, and Magazine Release Button straw colored.

MODEL:	Type 14 Year (1925)
MANUFACTURER:	Nagoya Army Ordnance; Nambu Factory.
SIGHTS:	Front — Dove Tail Blade.
	Rear — Undercut Notch.
GRIPS:	Serrated Mahogany.
SAFETY:	Manual Thumb — Left side.
DESIGNATION:	Japanese Armed Forces Model, primarily Army,
	but has appeared with Naval markings.

MARKINGS

CHAMBER:	None.
FRAME:	Year and Month of manufacture (1938 - March),
	Character for *"Showa,"* inspection stamp.
RECEIVER:	Serial Number and Nagoya Arsenal Symbol with first
	Character of name *"Nambu."*
DISTINCTIVE FEATURES:	Fine blued finish and workmanship. Aluminum Bottom
	nickel-plated Magazine. Safety Lever, Trigger, Sear Bar,
	and Magazine Release Button straw colored.

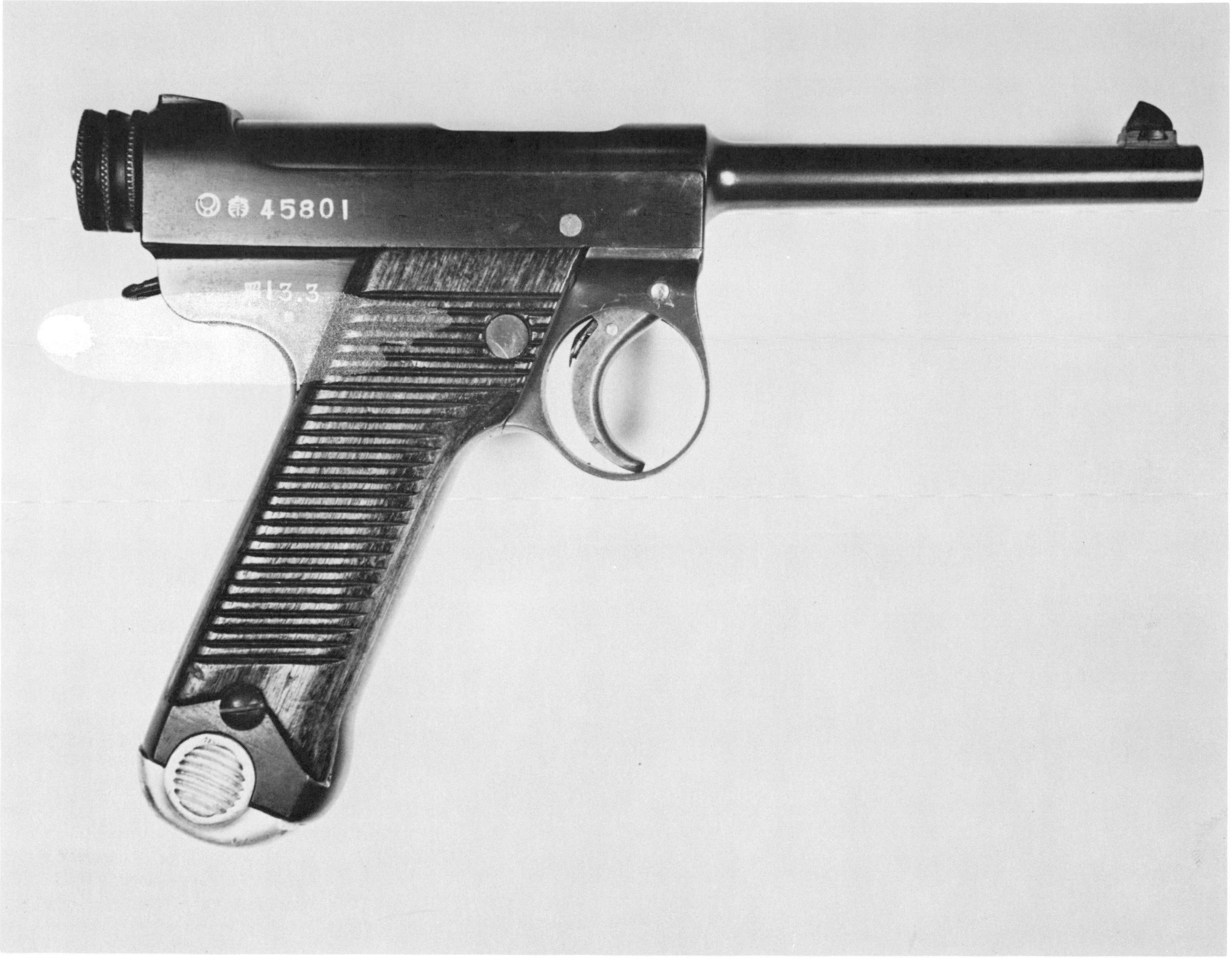
45801
13.3

MODEL: Type 14 Year (1925)

MANUFACTURER: Nagoya Army Ordnance; Nambu Factory.

SIGHTS: Front — Dove Tail Blade.

Rear — Undercut Notch.

GRIPS: Serrated Mahogany.

SAFETY: Manual Thumb — Left side.

DESIGNATION. Japanese Armed Forces Model, primarily Army, but has appeared with Naval markings.

MARKINGS

CHAMBER: None.

FRAME: Year and Month of manufacture (1939 - September), Character for *"Showa,"* and inspection stamp.

RECEIVER: Serial Number and Nagoya Arsenal Symbol with first Character of name *"Nambu."*

DISTINCTIVE FEATURES: Excellent blued finish and workmanship. Magazine has pot-metal bottom. This is last model with small Trigger Guard. Safety Lever, Trigger, Sear Bar and Magazine Release Button straw colored.

MODEL: Type 14 Year (1925)
MANUFACTURER: Nagoya Army Ordnance, Nambu Factory.
SIGHTS: Front — Dove Tail Blade.
Rear — Undercut Notch.
SAFETY: Serrated Mahogany.
GRIPS: Manual Thumb — Left side.
DESIGNATION: Japanese Armed Forces Model, primarily Army, but has appeared with Naval markings.

MARKINGS

CHAMBER: None.
FRAME: Year and Month of manufacture (1939 - December), Character for *"Showa,"* and inspection stamp.
RECEIVER: Serial Number and Nagoya Arsenal Symbol with first Character of name *"Nambu."*
DISTINCTIVE FEATURES: First model with Large Trigger Guard. This example is known as Transition Model as it was also produced in this year with Small Trigger Guard. Still retained excellent blued finish and workmanship. Aluminum Bottom nickel-plated Magazine. Safety Lever, Trigger, Sear Bar, and Magazine Release Button straw colored.

MODEL: Type 14 Year (1925)

MANUFACTURER: Nagoya Army Ordnance; Nambu Factory.

SIGHTS: Front — Dove Tail Blade.

Rear — Undercut Notch.

GRIPS: Serrated Mahogany.

SAFETY: Manual Thumb — Left side.

DESIGNATION: Japanese Armed Forces Model, primarily Army, but has appeared with Naval markings.

MARKINGS

CHAMBER: None.

FRAME: Year and Month of manufacture (1940 - December), Character for *"Showa,"* and inspection stamp.

RECEIVER: Serial Number and Nagoya Arsenal Symbol with first Character of name *"Nambu."*

DISTINCTIVE FEATURES: Magazine Bottom pot-metal. First example with Magazine Follower Release Spring. All Magazines from this year on had small notch in front near bottom to allow this spring to disengage Follower after insertion into pistol. Excellent blued finish and general workmanship. Safety Lever, Sear Bar, Trigger, and Magazine Release Button straw colored.

MODEL:	Type 14 Year (1925)
MANUFACTURER:	Nagoya Army Ordnance; Nambu Factory.
SIGHTS:	Front — Dove Tail Blade.
	Rear — Undercut Notch.
GRIPS:	Serrated Mahogany.
SAFETY:	Manual Thumb — Left side.
DESIGNATION:	Japanese Armed Forces Model, primarily Army, but has appeared with Naval markings.

MARKINGS

CHAMBER:	None.
FRAME:	Year and Month of manufacture (1941 - August), Character for *"Showa,"* and inspection stamp.
RECEIVER:	Serial Number and Nagoya Arsenal Symbol with first Character of name *"Nambu."*
DISTINCTIVE FEATURES:	Magazine bottom pot-metal. Safety Lever, Sear Bar, Trigger, and Magazine Release Button straw colored. Very good blued finish and workmanship.

MODEL: Type 14 Year (1925)

MANUFACTURER: Nagoya Arsenal.

SIGHTS: Front — Dove Tail Blade.

Rear — Undercut Notch.

GRIPS: Serrated Mahogany.

SAFETY: Manual Thumb — Left side.

DESIGNATION: Japanese Armed Forces Model, primarily Army, but has appeared with Naval markings.

MARKINGS

CHAMBER: None.

FRAME: Year and Month of manufacture (1942 - August), Character for *"Showa,"* and inspection stamp.

RECEIVER: Serial Number and Symbol of Nagoya Arsenal with an Inspector General's Symbol to denote in which district it was produced, on right side. Area "A".

DISTINCTIVE FEATURES: This year is when the pressure of the war effort made itself felt in the Japanese arms industry. This model is the first with Shortened Firing Pin, due to shortage of high-grade steel. Also, Magazine is blued rather than nickel-plated. Safety Lever, Sear Bar, Trigger, Magazine Release Button, and even Bolt and Extractor all blued. General blued finish and workmanship is good, but beginning to show strain around the edges.

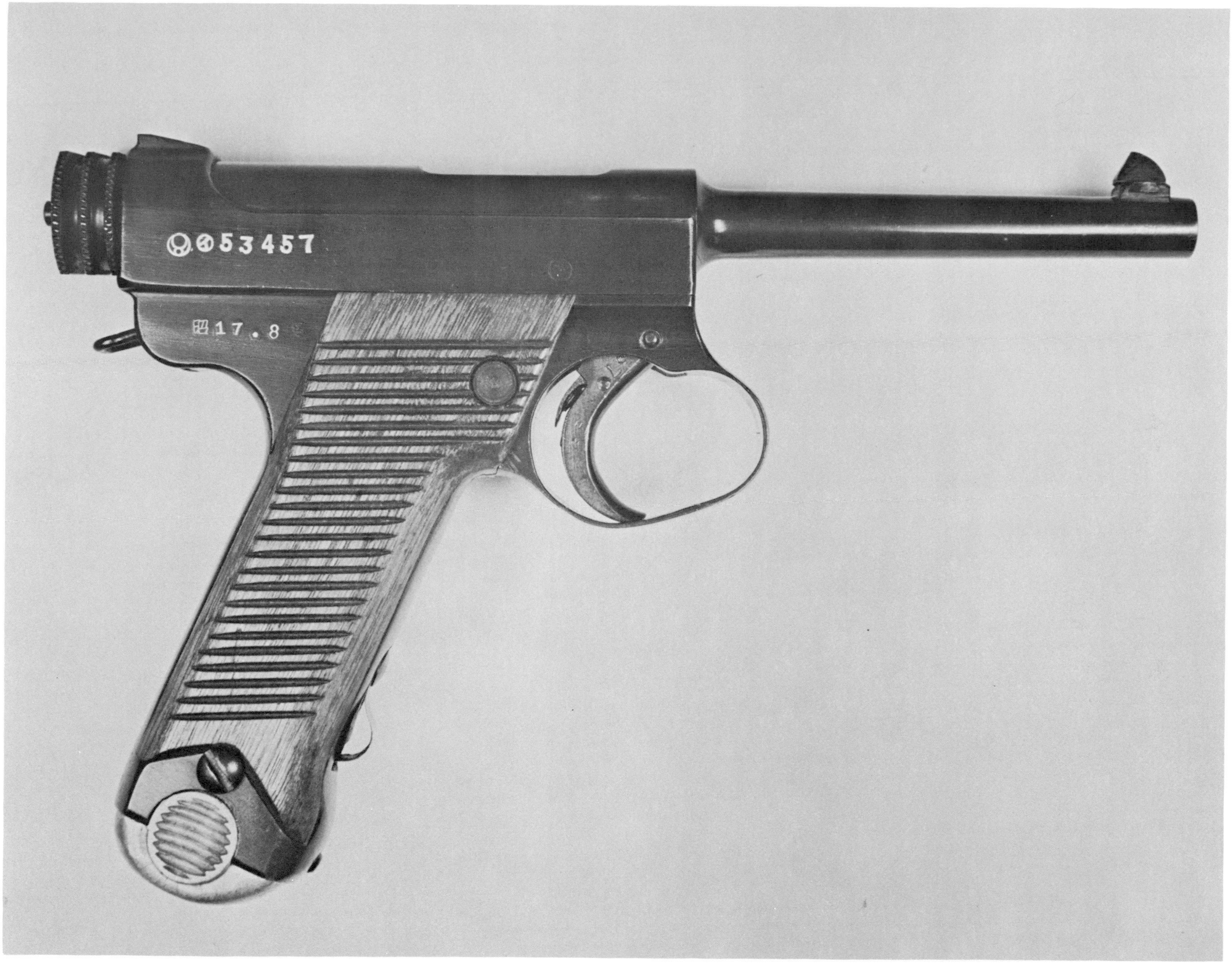
53457
17.8

MODEL: Type 14 Year (1925)

MANUFACTURER: Nagoya Army Ordnance; Nambu Factory.

SIGHTS: Front — Dove Tail Blade.

Rear — Undercut Notch.

GRIPS: Serrated Mahogany.

SAFETY: Manual Thumb — Left side.

DESIGNATION: Japanese Armed Forces Model, primarily Army, but has appeared with Naval markings.

MARKINGS

CHAMBER: None.

FRAME: Year and Month of manufacture (1942 - August), Character for *"Showa,"* and inspection stamp.

RECEIVER: Serial Number and Symbol of Nagoya Arsenal with first Character of name *"Nambu"* and Inspector General's Symbol on right side. Area "A".

DISTINCTIVE FEATURES: This example differs from Nagoya manufactured model in that the Safety Lever, Sear Bar, Trigger, and Magazine Release Button are still straw colored. Evidently the old craftsmen were reluctant to give in to the pressure of war production. Blued finish and workmanship still good, but machining marks beginning to show.

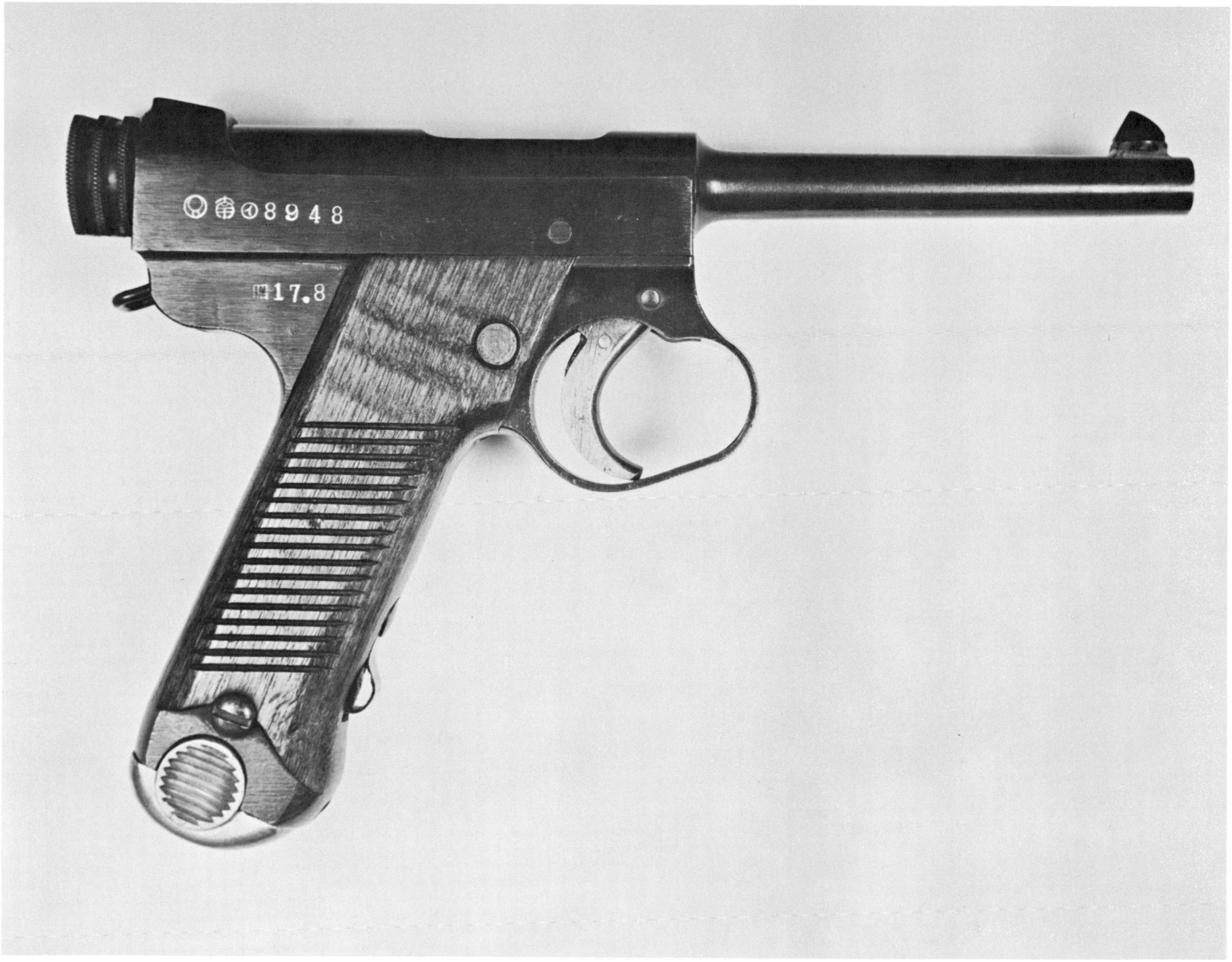
8948
17.8

MODEL:	Type 14 Year (1925)
MANUFACTURER:	Nagoya Army Ordnance; Nambu Factory.
SIGHTS:	Front — Dove Tail Blade.
	Rear — Undercut Notch.
GRIPS:	Serrated Mahogany.
SAFETY:	Manual Thumb — Left side.
DESIGNATION:	Japanese Armed Forces Model, primarily Army, but has appeared with Naval markings.

MARKINGS

CHAMBER:	None.
FRAME:	Year and Month of manufacture (1943 - July), Character for *"Showa,"* and inspection stamp.
RECEIVER:	Serial Number and Symbol of Nagoya Arsenal with first Character of name *"Nambu"* and inspector General's Symbol on right side. Area "A".
DISTINCTIVE FEATURES:	This example again differs from Nagoya manufactured model, with Safety Lever, Sear Bar, Trigger, and Magazine Release Button retaining straw color.

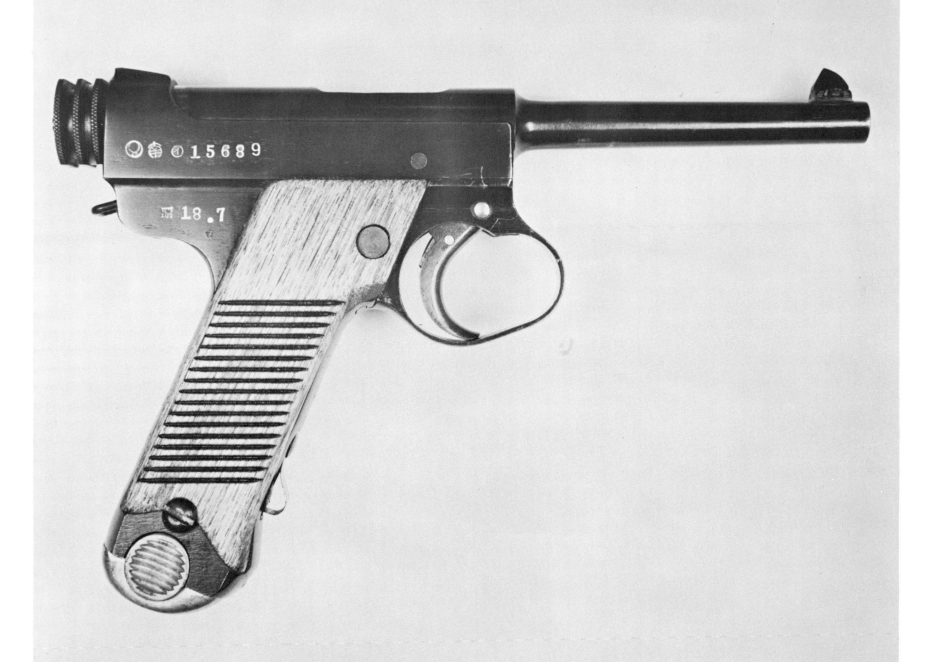

MODEL:	Type 14 Year (1925)
MANUFACTURER:	Nagoya Arsenal.
SAFETY:	Front — Dove Tail Blade.
	Rear — Undercut Notch.
GRIPS:	Serrated Mahogany.
SAFETY:	Manual Thumb — Left side.
DESIGNATION:	Japanese Armed Forces Model, primarily Army, but has appeared with Naval markings.

MARKINGS

CHAMBER:	None.
FRAME:	Year and Month of manufacture (1943 - November), Character for *"Showa,"* and inspection stamp.
RECEIVER:	Serial Number and Symbol of Nagoya Arsenal with Inspector General's Symbol. Area "A".
DISTINCTIVE FEATURES:	All parts blued on this example except Bolt. Blued finish still deep but machining marks more evident. Bolt flame-hardened in critical wear areas, rather than all-hardened, as had been the case previous to this year.

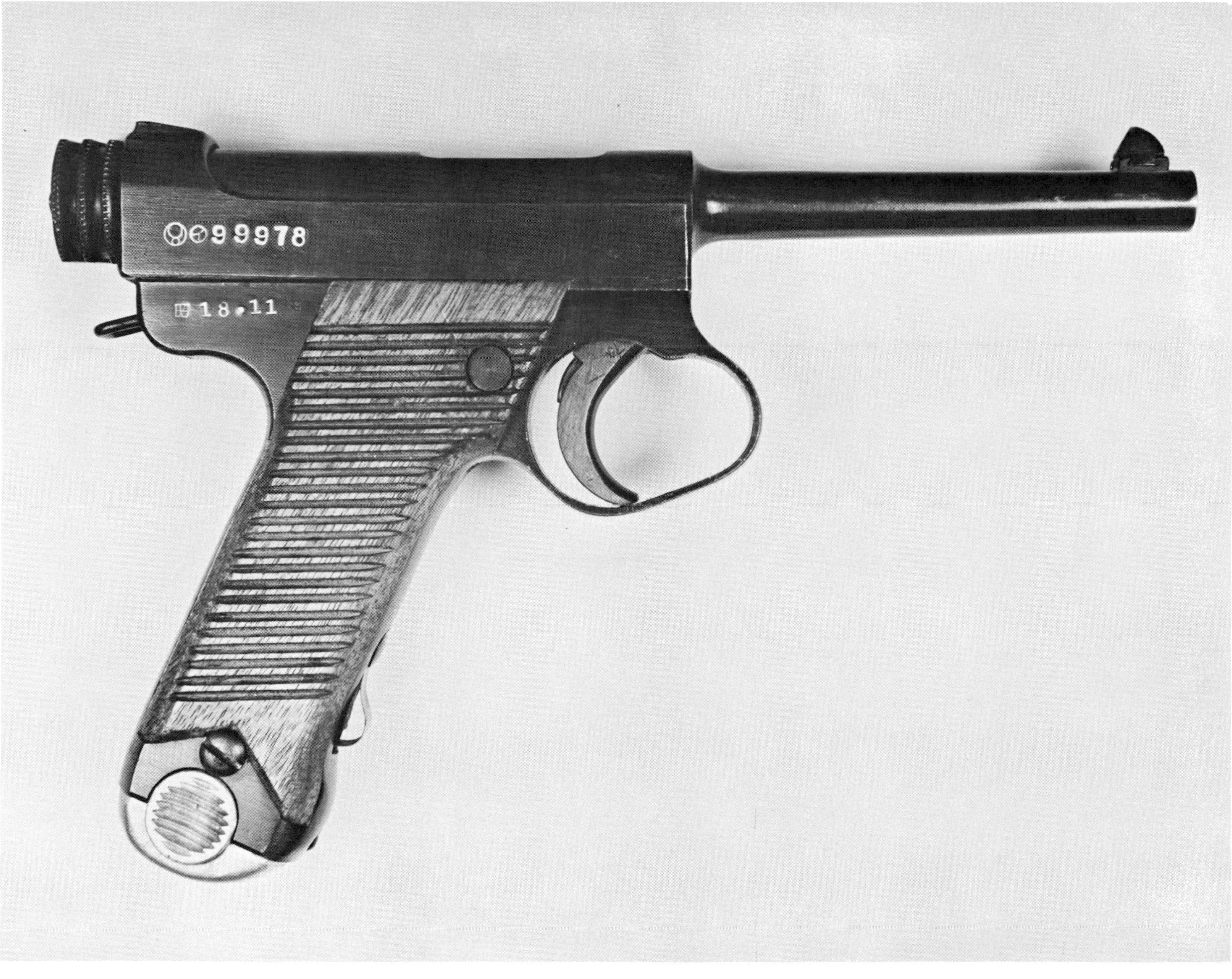
99978
18.11

MODEL:	Type 14 Year (1925)
MANUFACTURER:	Nagoya Arsenal.
SIGHTS:	Front — Dove Tail Blade.
	Rear — Undercut Notch.
GRIPS:	Serrated Mahogany.
SAFETY:	Manual Thumb — Left side.
DESIGNATION:	Japanese Armed Forces Model, primarily Army, but has appeared with Naval markings.

MARKINGS

CHAMBER:	None.
FRAME:	Year and Month of manufacture (1944 - January), Character for *"Showa,"* and inspection stamp.
RECEIVER:	Serial Number and Symbol of Nagoya Arsenal with Inspector General's Symbol. Area "B".
DISTINCTIVE FEATURES:	All parts blued except Bolt. This was first year with solid knurled Cocking Piece. This particular example has a much finer knurl than appears on later models of same year. Blueing becoming thin and machining marks more pronounced.

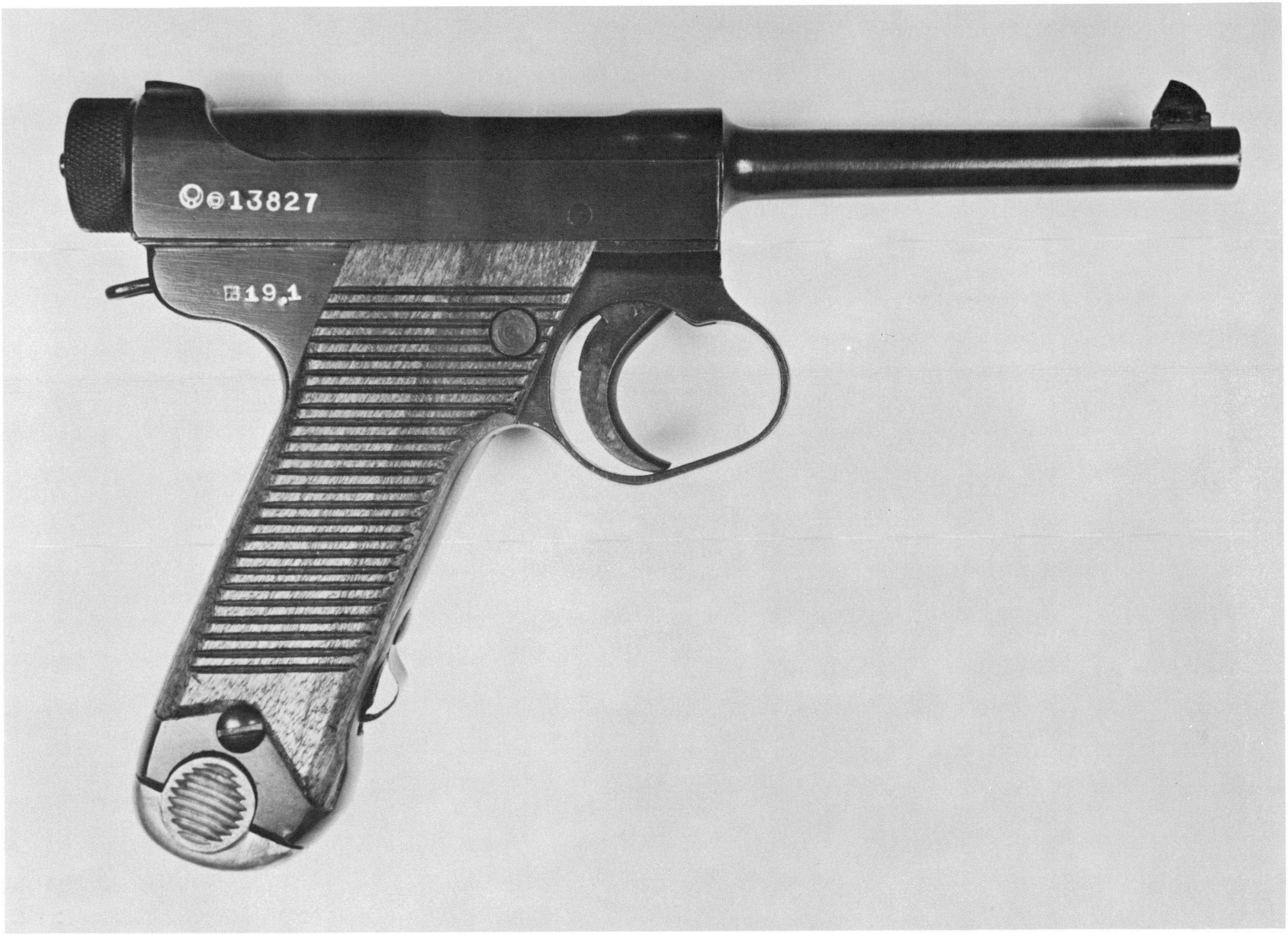
13827
19.1

MODEL:	Type 14 year (1925)
MANUFACTURER:	Nagoya Arsenal.
SIGHTS:	Front — Dove Tail Blade.
	Rear — Undercut Notch.
GRIPS:	Serrated Mahogany.
SAFETY:	Manual Thumb — Left side.
DESIGNATION:	Japanese Armed Forces Model, primarily Army, but has appeared with Naval markings.

MARKINGS

CHAMBER:	None.
FRAME:	Year and Month of manufacture (1944-March), Character for "Showa," and inspection stamp.
RECEIVER:	Serial Number and Symbol of Nagoya Arsenal with Inspector General's Symbol. Area "B".
DISTINCTIVE FEATURES:	Identical to previous example dated 1944 January, except Cocking Piece has coarse knurl which prevailed until surrender stopped production.

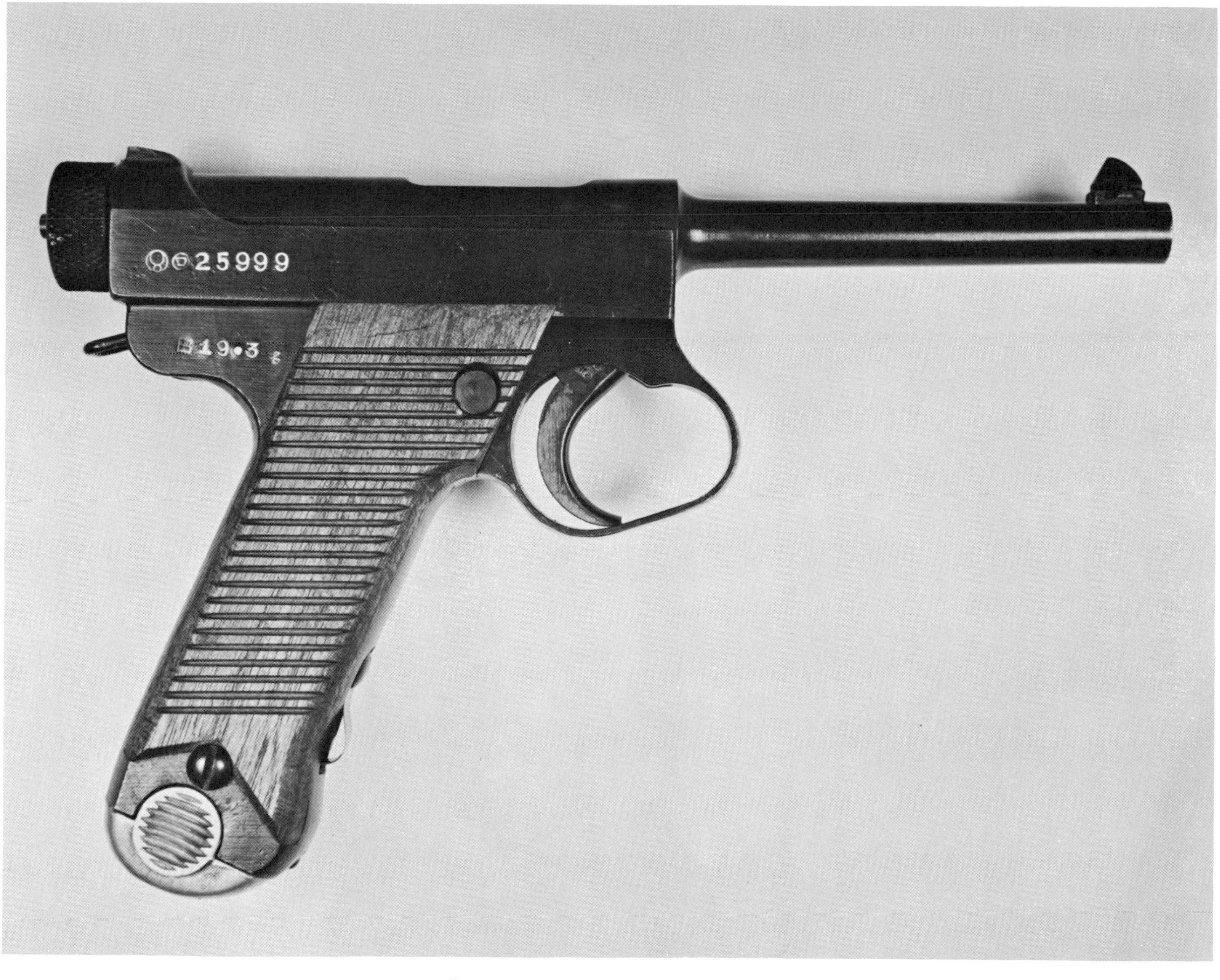
25999
19.3

MODEL:	Type 14 Year (1925)
MANUFACTURER:	Nagoya Arsenal.
SIGHTS:	Front — Dove Tail Blade.
	Rear — Undercut Notch.
GRIPS:	Smooth Mahogany.
SAFETY:	Manual Thumb — Left side.
DESIGNATION:	Japanese Armed Forces Model, primarily Army, but has appeared with Naval markings.

MARKINGS

CHAMBER:	None.
FRAME:	Year and Month of manufacture (1944-November), Character for "*Showa,*" and inspection stamp.
RECEIVER:	Serial Number and Symbol of Nagoya Arsenal with Inspector General's Symbol. Area "B".
DISTINCTIVE FEATURES:	Smooth flat Grips. All parts blued except Bolt. Blue getting thin and machining marks all over. Tolerances and fits very loose.

MODEL: Type 14 Year (1925)

MANUFACTURER: Nagoya Army Ordnance; Nambu Factory.

SIGHTS: Front — Dove Tail Blade.

Rear — Undercut Notch.

GRIPS: Serrated Mahogany.

SAFETY: Manual Thumb — Left side.

DESIGNATION: Japanese Armed Forces Model, primarily Army, but has appeared with Naval markings.

MARKINGS

CHAMBER: None.

FRAME: Year and Month of manufacture (1944-April), Character for *"Showa,"* and inspection stamp.

RECEIVER: Serial Number and Symbol of Nagoya Arsenal with first Character of name *"Nambu"* and Inspector General's Symbol on right side. Area "A".

DISTINCTIVE FEATURES: Grooved Cocking Piece. Safety Lever, Sear Bar, Trigger, and Magazine Release Button straw colored. Even at this late date the Nambu Works still tried to maintain some quality in the manufacturing of these pistols. Finish and machining good.

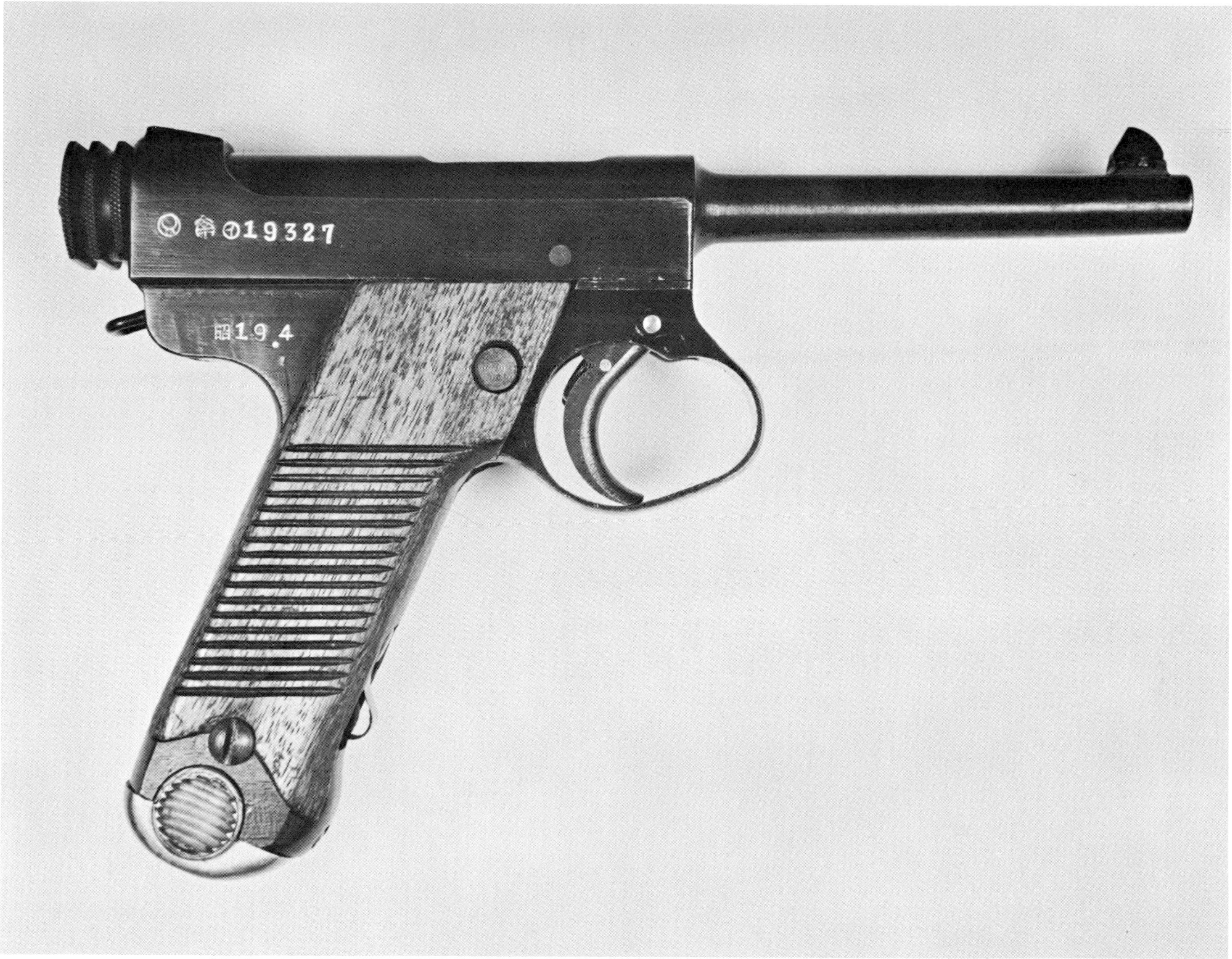
19327
昭19.4

MODEL: Type 14 Year (1925)
MANUFACTURER: Nagoya Arsenal.
SIGHTS: Front — Dove Tail Blade.
Rear — Undercut Notch.
GRIPS: Smooth Mahogany.
SAFETY: Manual Thumb — Left side.
DESIGNATION: Japanese Armed Forces Model, primarily Army, but has appeared with Naval markings.

MARKINGS

CHAMBER: None.
FRAME: Year and Month of manufacture (1945 - March), Character for "Showa," and inspection stamp.
RECEIVER: Serial Number and Symbol of Nagoya Arsenal with Inspector General's Symbol. Area "B".
DISTINCTIVE FEATURES: Smooth Grips. All parts blued except Bolt. This was the last year of production, this example being produced just six months before the formal surrender. By this time no pride or care was taken in the manufacture of weapons. The finish and workmanship are terrible. Rough machining marks have replaced finish machining marks. The order of the day was quantity, not quality.

Type 94
8mm pistol,
model 34

This pistol was originally produced for commercial sale and export. A dangerous design feature of an exposed sear led to poor sales on the commercial market, but when the war began it was adopted for military use. Production of this pistol, despite the exposed sear, continued up to the end of the war and even exceeded that of the Type 14 (1925) pistol in the closing months of the conflict.

Design type: Recoil operated, locked slide.

Weight with empty magazine: 1 pound, 11 ounces.

Overall length: 7.2 inches.

Barrel length: 3.8 inches.

Number of grooves: 6.

Direction of twist: Right.

Magazine capacity: 6 rounds.

Magazine weight: 5.5 ounces.

Design of parts and assembly reflects attention given to ease of manufacture. Dismounting procedure is as follows:

Draw the slide to the rear until it catches behind the magazine follower. Grasp the pistol in the right hand with the thumb under the rear of the frame and the fingers over the slide. Draw the slide back all the way and grip it tightly with the right hand. The slide is made in two pieces; the rear slide extension cocking piece being held in place by a transverse locking block which in turn is held in place by the firing pin, in its normal or rearward position. To remove the locking block, insert the left index finger into the hollow underside of the cocking piece and push the firing pin forward into the firing position. The locking block may now be pushed out from the right to the left. The locking block is rather small; it may be necessary to complete its removal with the aid of a punch. The cocking piece is now free and may be removed directly to the rear. Then with the left hand around the forward end of the slide, withdraw the magazine and ease the slide forward into the locked position. A slight pressure of the left thumb on the muzzle will unlock the slide and the remaining compression of the recoil spring will push the slide off the frame. The recoil spring and bushing will come with it. The barrel and lock may be lifted up and out of the frame.

**Parts
List**

TYPE 94 8mm PISTOL, MODEL 34

1. Frame
2. Sear Pivot Pin
3. Extractor
4. Bolt
5. Firing Pin
6. Firing Pin Return Spring
7. Sear Return Spring
8. Sear Bar
9. Trigger Pivot Pin
10. Hammer Pivot Pin
11. Safety Lever
12. Grip Stock — Left shown
13. Grip Stock
14. Grip Screw
15. Grip Screw

16. Hammer Spring
17. Hammer
18. Cocking Roller Pin
19. Cocking Roller
20. Barrel Locking Block
21. Barrel
22. Recoil Spring Bushing
23. Recoil Spring
24. Bolt Lock
25. Receiver & Barrel Housing
26. Magazine Safety Block
27. Magazine Safety Lever
28. Magazine Safety Return Spring
29. Magazine Safety Lever Nut
30. Magazine Safety Lever Spring
31. Trigger
32. Disconnector Pin
33. Disconnector Spring
34. Disconnector Body
35. Trigger Return Spring
36. Magazine Body
37. Magazine Base Plate
38. Magazine Spring
39. Magazine Follower
40. Loading Button

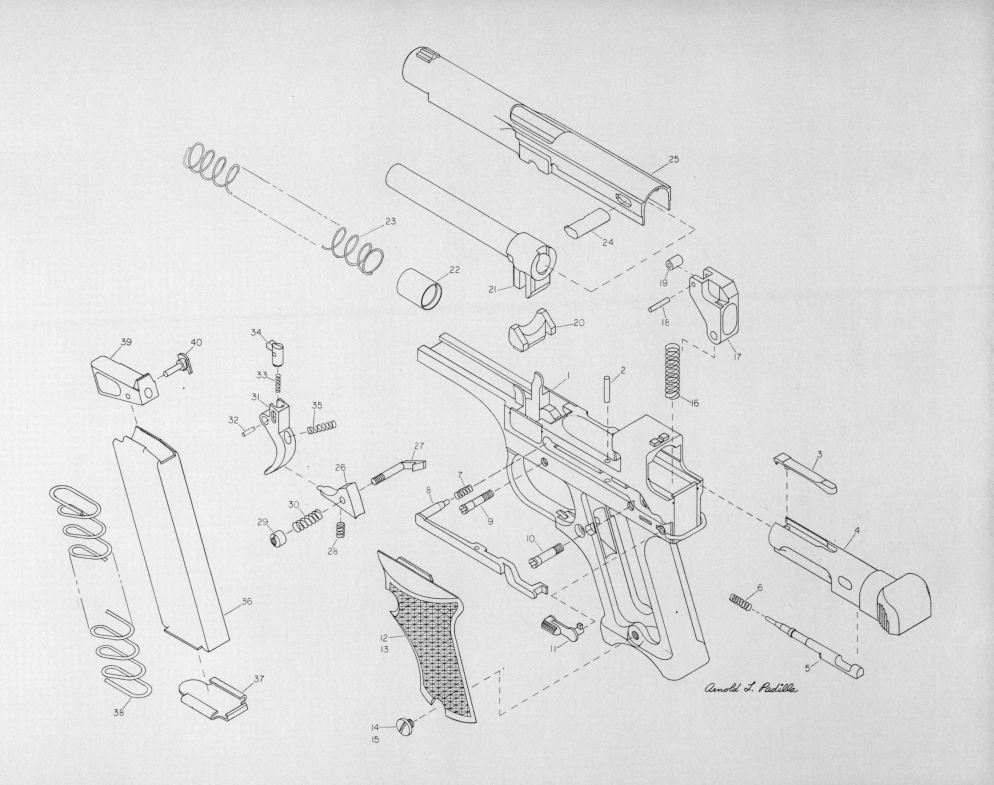

Arnold L. Padilla

MODEL: Type 94 (Commercial Designation Automatic Pistol Type B)

MANUFACTURER: Nambu Seisakusho (Toriimatsu Factory at Nagoya Arsenal).

SIGHTS: Front — Dovetailed inverted "V" Blade; Rear Square Notch.

GRIPS: Molded Black Plastic.

SAFETY: Manual — Cams sear out of engagement.
Magazine — Block against toe of Trigger.

DESIGNATION: Commercial Sale & Export Model.

MARKINGS

CHAMBER: None.

FRAME: Right Side — Serial No., Date of Manufacture, and
Manufacturer's Identification. (1937, September).
Left Side — Model Identification.

RECEIVER: None.

DISTINCTIVE FEATURES: Excellent finish and machining. Old style bluing.
Manual Safety straw colored. Magazine nickel plated.

MODEL: Type 94 (Commercial Designation Automatic Pistol Type B)
MANUFACTURER: Nambu Seisakusho (Toriimatsu Factory at Nagoya Arsenal).
SIGHTS: Front — Dovetailed inverted "V" Blade; Rear — Square Notch.
GRIPS: Molded Black Plastic.
SAFETY: Manual — Cams sear out of engagement.
Magazine — Block against toe of Trigger.
DESIGNATION: Commercial Sale & Export Model.

MARKINGS

CHAMBER: None.
FRAME: Right Side — Serial No., Date of Manufacture,
and Manufacturer's Identification. (1938, May).
Left Side — Model Identification.
RECEIVER: None.
DISTINCTIVE FEATURES: Excellent finish and machining. Old style bluing.
Manual Safety straw colored. Magazine nickel plated.

MODEL: Type 94 (Commercial Designation Automatic Pistol Type B)
MANUFACTURER: Nambu Seisakusho (Toriimatsu Factory at Nagoya Arsenal).
SIGHTS: Front — Dovetailed inverted "V" Blade; Rear — Square Notch.
GRIPS: Molded Black Plastic.
SAFETY: Manual — Cams sear out of engagement.
Magazine — Block against toe of Trigger.
DESIGNATION: Commercial Sale & Export Model.

MARKINGS

CHAMBER: None.
FRAME: Right Side — Serial No., Date of Manufacture,
and Manufacturer's Identification. (1939, December).
Left Side — Model Identification.
RECEIVER: None.
DISTINCTIVE FEATURES: Excellent finish and machining. Old style bluing.
Manual Safety straw colored. Magazine nickel plated.

MODEL: Model 94 (1934)

MANUFACTURER: Nambu Selsakusho (Toriimatsu Factory at Nagoya Arsenal).

SIGHTS: Front — Dovetailed inverted "V" Blade;

Rear — Square Notch.

GRIPS: Molded Black Plastic.

SAFETY: Manual — Cams sear out of engagement.

Magazine — Block against toe of Trigger.

DESIGNATION: Japanese Service Model, for Ground and Air Force Units.
Withdrawn from commercial sales due to poor sales record.
Bad design feature of exposed Sear Bar undoubtedly
one of principal reasons for buyer rejection.

MARKINGS

CHAMBER: None.

FRAME: Right Side — Serial No., Date of Manufacture,
and Manufacturer's Identification. (1940, July).
Left Side — Model Identification.

RECEIVER: None.

DISTINCTIVE FEATURES: Quality of machining and finish beginning to fall off.
Trigger and Manual Safety straw colored.
Magazine nickel plated.

MODEL: Type 94 (Commercial Designation Automatic Pistol Type B)
MANUFACTURER: Nambu Seisakusho (Toriimatsu Factory at Nagoya Arsenal).
SIGHTS: Front — Dovetailed inverted "V" Blade; Rear Square Notch.
GRIPS: Molded Black Plastic.
SAFETY: Manual — Cams sear out of engagement.
Magazine — Block against toe of Trigger.
DESIGNATION: Japanese Service Model.

MARKINGS

CHAMBER: None.
FRAME: Right Side — Serial No., Date of Manufacture,
and Manufacturer's Identification. (1941, February).
Left Side — Model Identification.
RECEIVER: None.
DISTINCTIVE FEATURES: Machining and finish mediocre. Trigger and
Manual Safety straw colored. Magazine nickel plated.

MODEL:	Type 94 (Commercial Designation Automatic Pistol Type B)
MANUFACTURER:	Nambu Seisakusho (Toriimatsu Factory at Nagoya Arsenal).
SIGHTS:	Front — Dovetailed inverted "V" Blade; Rear — Square Notch.
GRIPS:	Molded Black Plastic.
SAFETY:	Manual — Cams sear out of engagement.
	Magazine — Block against toe of Trigger.
DESIGNATION:	Japanese Service Model.

MARKINGS

CHAMBER:	None.
FRAME:	Right Side — Serial No., Date of Manufacture, and Manufacturer's Identification. (1942, December). Left Side — Model Identification.
RECEIVER:	None.
DISTINCTIVE FEATURES:	Finish and machining steadily becoming worse. Tool marks showing. Smooth only on areas readily accessible. Trigger and Manual Safety straw colored. Magazine blued.

MODEL: Type 94 (Commercial Designation Automatic Pistol Type B)

MANUFACTURER: Nambu Seisakusho (Toriimatsu Factory at Nagoya Arsenal).

SIGHTS: Front — Dovetailed inverted "V" Blade; Rear — Square Notch.

GRIPS: Molded Black Plastic.

SAFETY: Manual — Cams sear out of engagement.
Magazine — Block against toe of Trigger.

DESIGNATION: Japanese Service Model.

MARKINGS

CHAMBER: None.

FRAME: Right Side — Serial No., Date of Manufacture,
and Manufacturer's Identification. (1943, April).
Left Side — Model Identification.

RECEIVER: None.

DISTINCTIVE FEATURES: Finish poor. Machining rough. Fit becoming loose
and sloppy. Trigger and Manual Safety straw colored.
Magazine blued.

MODEL: Type 94 (Commercial Designation Automatic Pistol Type B)
MANUFACTURER: Nambu Seisakusho (Toriimatsu Factory at Nagoya Arsenal).
SIGHTS: Front — Dovetailed inverted "V" Blade; Rear — Square Notch.
GRIPS: Molded Black Plastic.
SAFETY: Manual — Cams sear out of engagement.
Magazine — Block against toe of Trigger.
DESIGNATION: Japanese Service Model.

MARKINGS

CHAMBER: None.
FRAME: Right Side — Serial No., Date of Manufacture,
and Manufacturer's Identification. (1944, May).
Left Side — Model Identification.
RECEIVER: None.
DISTINCTIVE FEATURES: Finish thin and poor. Machining very rough and shoddy.
Trigger and Manual Safety blued. Magazine blued.

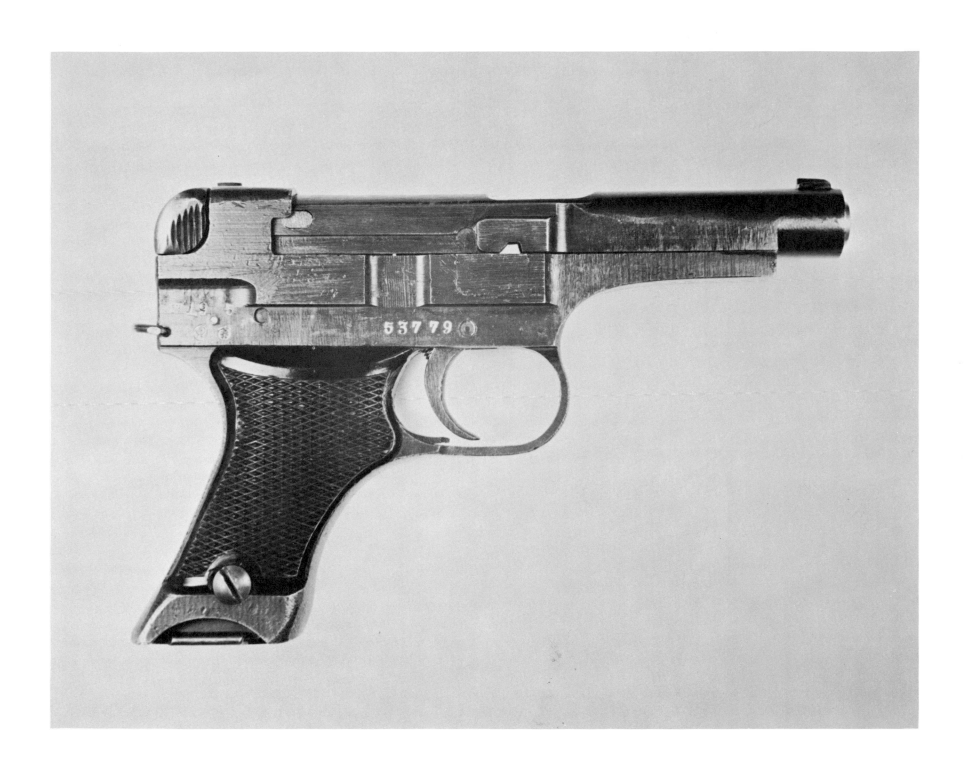

MODEL: Type 94 (Commercial Designation Automatic Pistol Type B)
MANUFACTURER: Nambu Seisakusho (Toriimatsu Factory at Nagoya Arsenal).
SIGHTS: Front — Dovetailed inverted "V" Blade; Rear — Square Notch.
GRIPS: Smooth flat Mahogany.
SAFETY: Manual — Cams sear out of engagement.
Magazine — Block against toe of Trigger.
DESIGNATION: Japanese Service Model.

MARKINGS

CHAMBER: None.
FRAME: Right Side — Serial No., Date of Manufacture, and Manufacturer's Identification. (1944, December).
Left Side — Model Identification.
RECEIVER: None.
DISTINCTIVE FEATURES: Simplifying production techniques led to abandonment of plastic grips and any regard for finish or machining quality. Trigger and Manual Safety blued. Magazine blued.

MODEL: Type 94 (Commercial Designation Automatic Pistol Type B)
MANUFACTURER: Nambu Seisakusho (Toriimatsu Factory at Nagoya Arsenal).
SIGHTS: Front — Dovetailed inverted "V" Blade; Rear — Square Notch.
GRIPS: Flat Mahogany — Rough cut.
SAFETY: Manual — Cams sear out of engagement.
Magazine — Block against toe of Trigger.
DESIGNATION: Japanese Service Model.

MARKINGS

CHAMBER: None.
FRAME: Right Side — Serial No., Date of Manufacture,
and Manufacturer's Identification. (1945, January).
Left Side — Model Identification.
RECEIVER: None.
DISTINCTIVE FEATURES: Absolutely the worst example of firearm manufacturing
seen; finish so thin it can be seen through, machining
roughest ever seen, fits rattle, tolerances looser.
Trigger and Manual Safety blued. Magazine blued.

Miscellany

Top: View showing transition model of new style flat sear bar. New year 1940.

Bottom: View showing transition model of old style sear bar. Old year 1939.

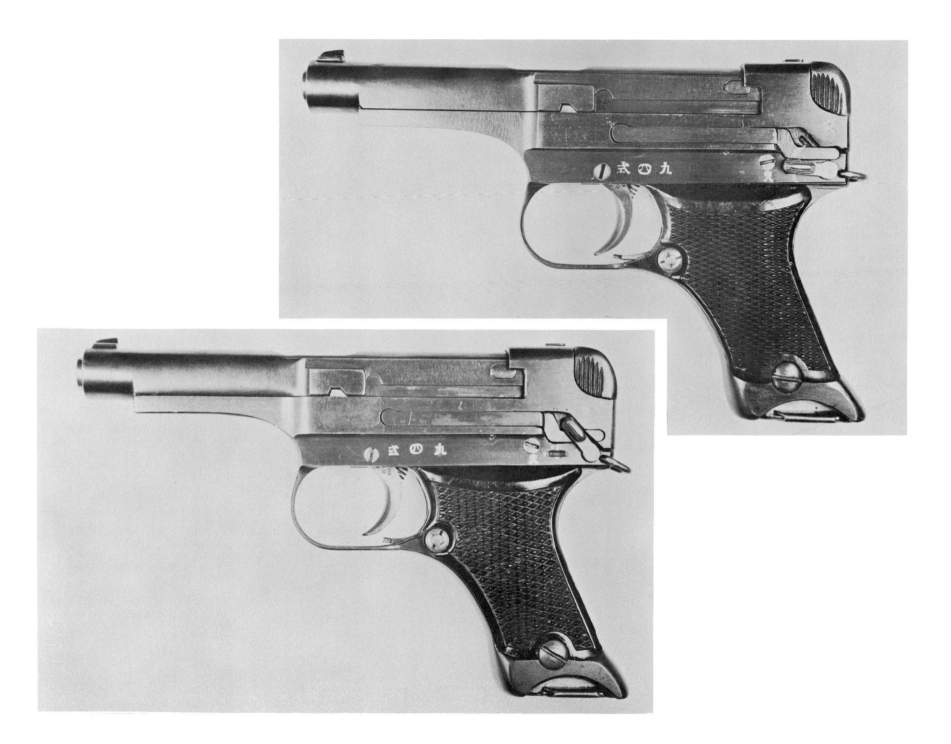

MAGAZINES

1. 1904 Production — Wood base — nickel plated
2. "Papa" 8mm — Aluminum base — nickel plated
3. "Baby" 7mm — Aluminum base — nickel plated

CLEANING RODS

1. Model 26 Revolver
2. Model 14 Early type — nickel plated
3. Model 14 Late type — blued
4. Model 14 Last type — blued

MAGAZINES — Model 94 (1934)

1. Early type — nickel plated
2. Late type — blued
3. Last type — blued

MAGAZINES — Model 14 (1925)

1. Early type — Aluminum base — nickel plated
2. Late type — Pot-metal base — blued
3. Transition — Aluminum base — nickel plated

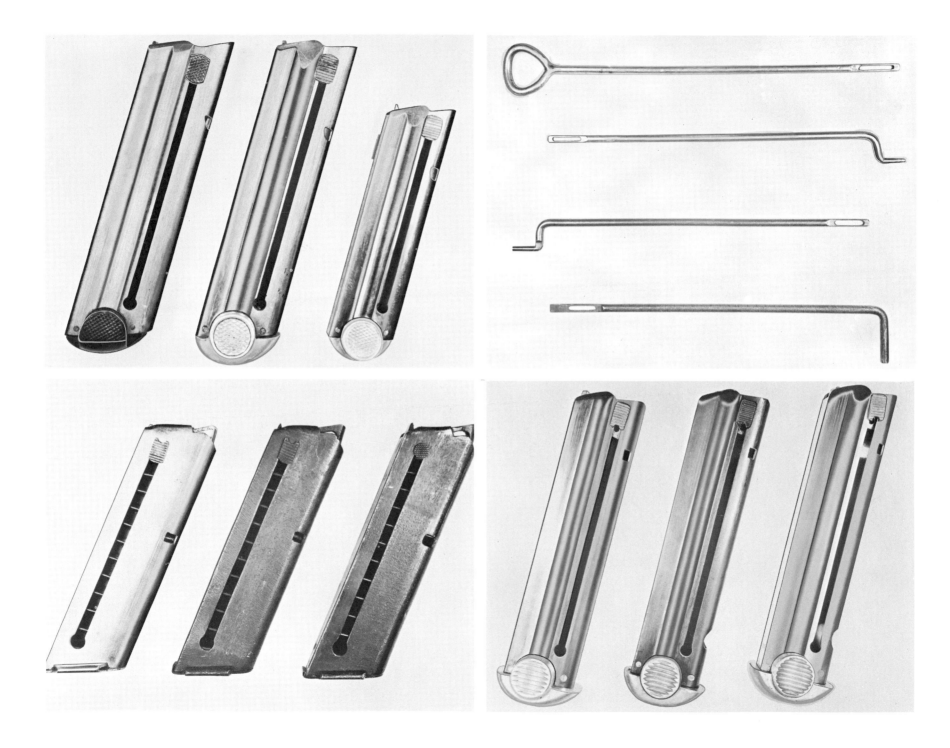

MODEL 26 (9mm) REVOLVER HOLSTER

Pouch has cartridge loops for 18 rounds. Cleaning rod stored in pocket along front. Well made of top-quality, brown finished cowhide.

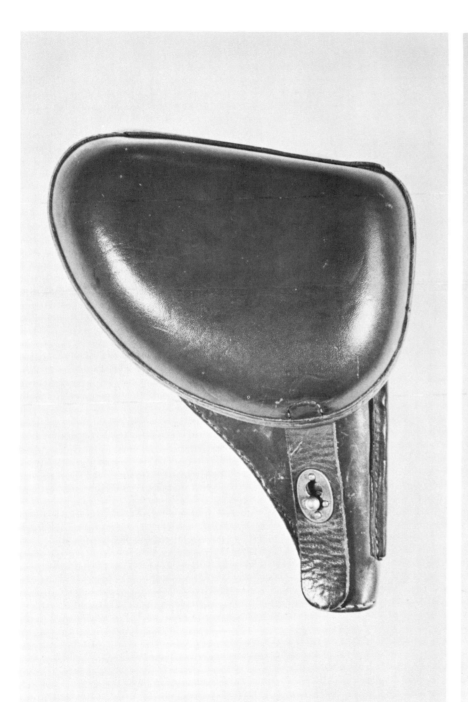 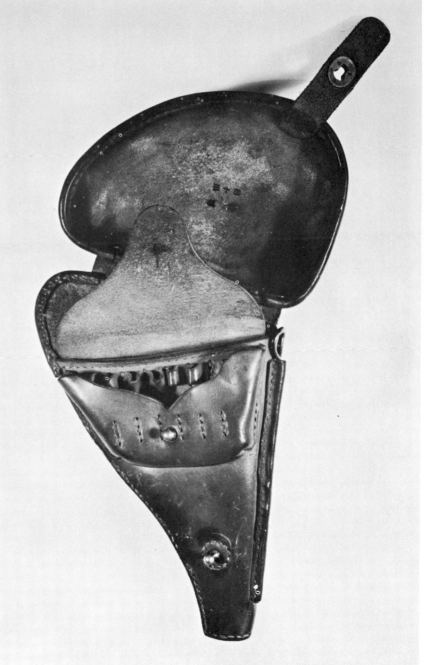

"PAPA" NAMBU HOLSTER
Pouch has cartridge loops for 16 rounds. Basically same as "Baby" holster. Cleaning rod and extra magazine stored internally in same fashion, only difference is size. Made of top-grade cowhide.

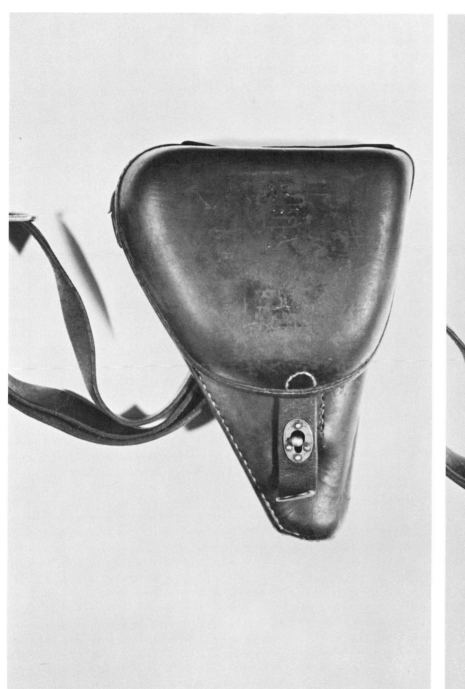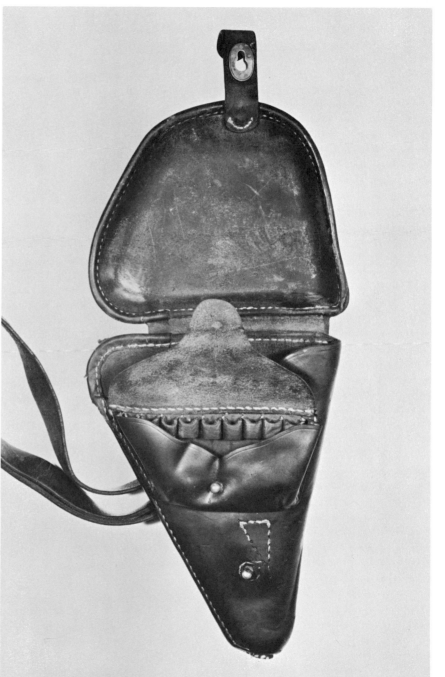

"BABY" NAMBU HOLSTER

Pouch has cartridge loops for 14 rounds. Cleaning rod stored inside along back seam, retained by small leather loop. These holsters have no separate magazine pouch, but space exists for storage in area formed below trigger guard and barrel. Top quality cowhide and excellent workmanship.

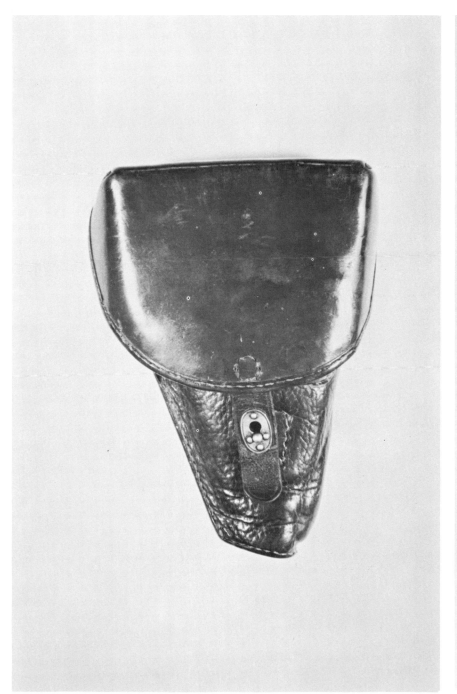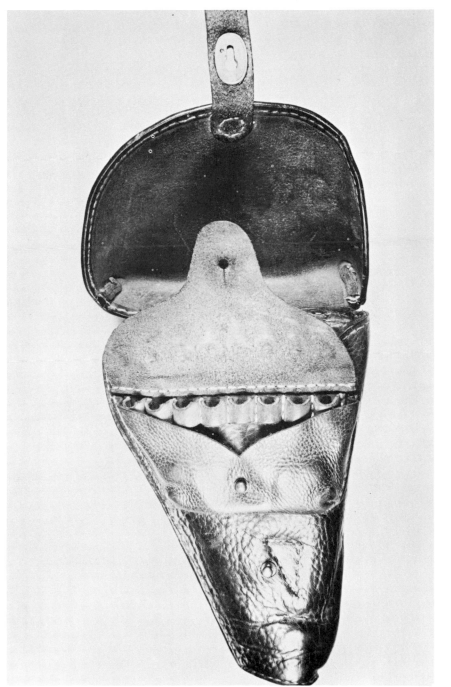

MODEL 14 (1925) HOLSTER—EARLY TYPE

Pouch contains 2 boxes of cartridges. Small pocket along front of cartridge pouch contains spare firing pin. Cleaning rod and extra magazine stored internally as in "Papa" and "Baby" holsters. Well made of top-grade cowhide.

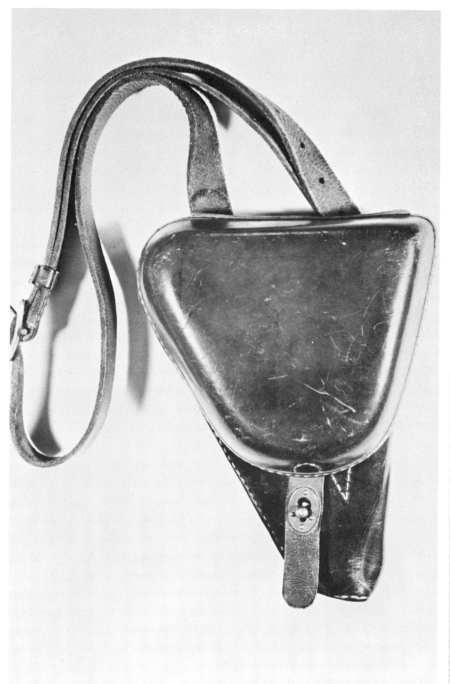

MODEL 14 (1925) HOLSTER—LATE TYPE

Same holster as early type except for material. This type is made from a molded rubberized fabric. Always found with large trigger guard model pistol. This is sometimes referred to as "Winter type" for that reason, but all pistols after 1941 were issued with this model holster regardless of location or season.

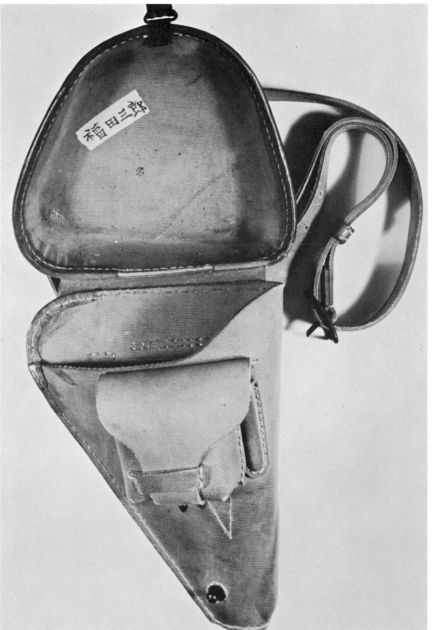

MODEL 94 (1934) HOLSTER

Pouch on front contains extra magazine and cleaning rod. Spare cartridges contained in separate pouch on shoulder strap. Well made of top-grade pigskin.

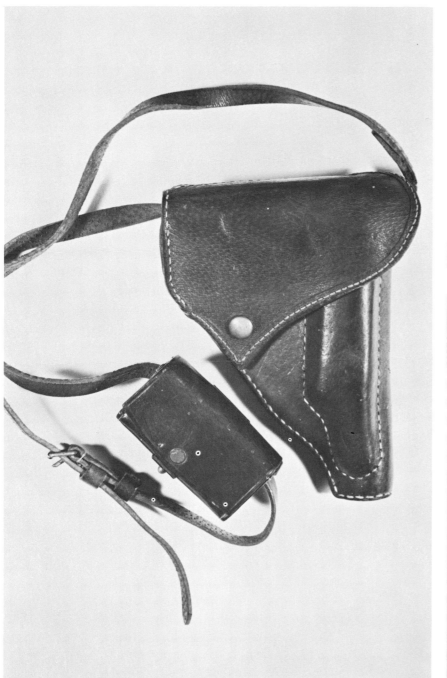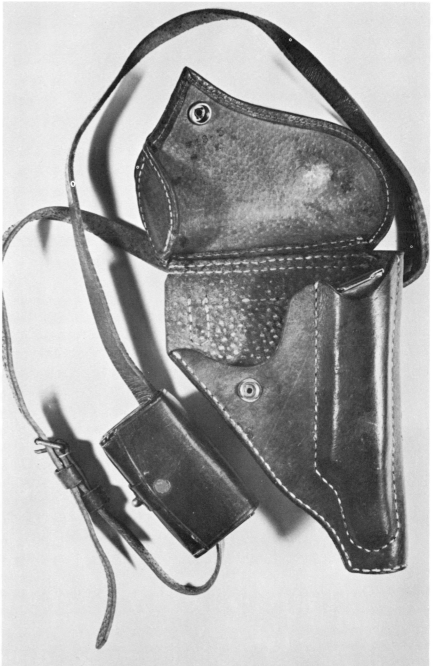

MODEL 94 (1934) HOLSTER—LATE TYPE

Same as early type except for small pouch containing spare firing pin and material. Constructed of a close weave, heavy grade canvas. Not often encountered, as material not suited to withstand tropical conditions.

Don Ovall Collection

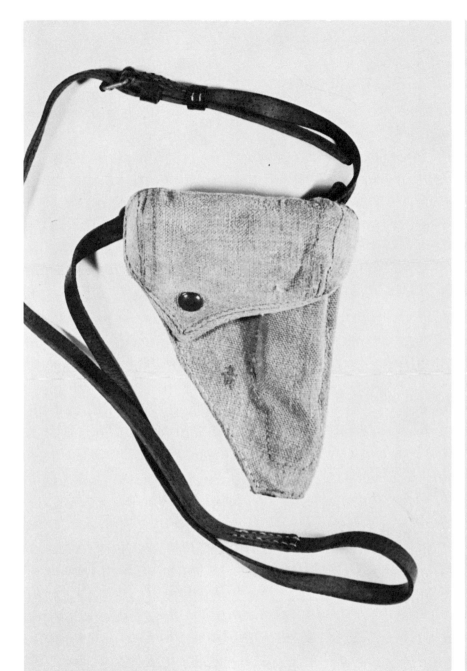
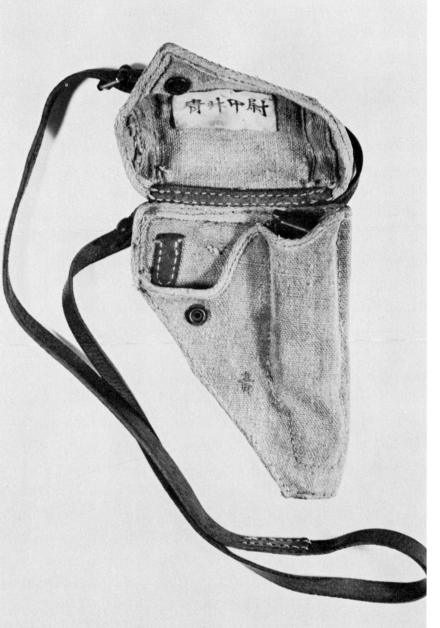

MODEL 1904 HOLSTER

No provision for extra magazine or cleaning rod. Excellent construction of top-grade brown pigskin. This specimen has piece of tape on outside with name and address of owner written on it. Appears to have been put on when owner turned pistol in to occupation troops at end of war.

MODEL 14 (1925) HOLSTER—EARLY TYPE

Same in all respects to other Model 14 except equipped with late type latch. Possibly the transition year model (leather to rubberized canvas material).

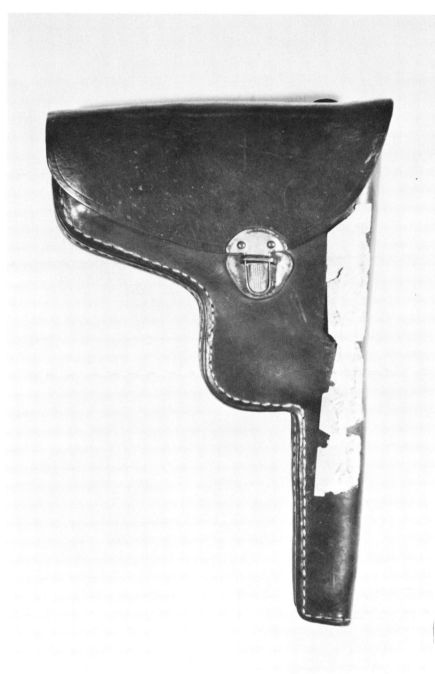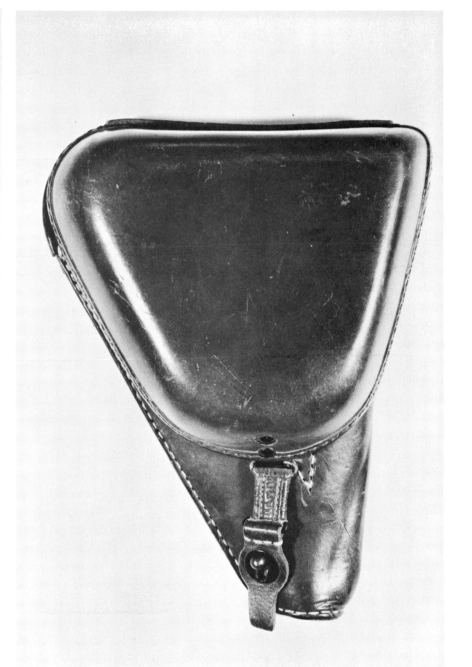

Typical box of cartridges. Box contains **15 rounds.**
Characters on top of box read: *"14th Year Type Pistol Bullet 15 pack."*

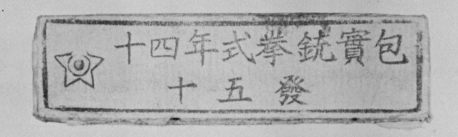

包實銃拳式年四十
發 五 十

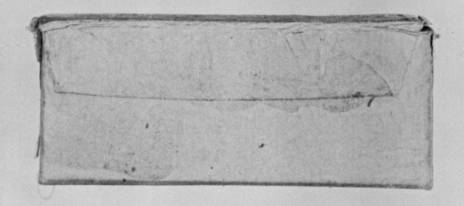

AMMUNITION

1. 8mm Standard Issue — copper jacketed.

2. 7mm Dummy.

3. 9mm Revolver Standard Issue — Lead.

4. 8mm Standard Issue — tin plated jacket.

5. 7mm Standard Issue — tin plated jacket.

6. 8mm Dummy.

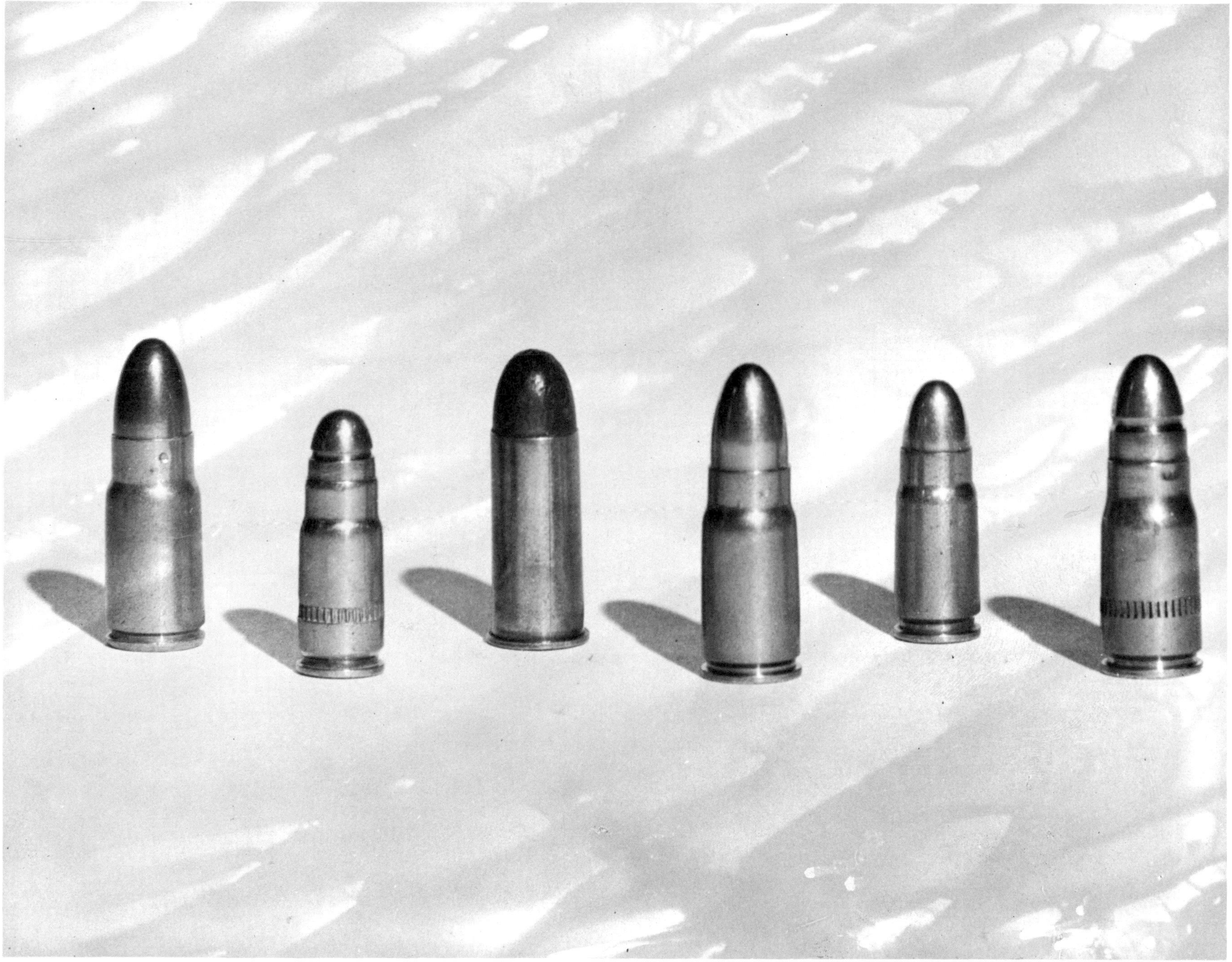

TYPE II HAMADA PISTOL

Designed in 1942 by Hamada Arms Shop under direction of Major Yato. Same basic functioning characteristics as Type 94. Accepted for service in June, 1943, and five hundred examples produced at Nagoya Arsenal after that date. Production version shown here.

Darel Magee Collection

NAMBU — EXPERIMENTAL

This is the 16-shot Nambu variation often heard of, but seldom seen. Although it retains some of the Nambu design features, it has the appearance of a Mauser-Lahti. It is evident that some effort was made to lighten the Receiver, but it still has a massively bulky look. With a full magazine, the over-all weight must have been formidable even by Western-World standards. The Grips are checkered Walnut; the Magazine Base is Aluminum. The specimen shown here bears the serial number 3, and was obtained from the Tokyo Arsenal. Other examples of this variation are known, with the lowest serial number being 1, the highest being 14.

Gary Cufley Collection

NAMBU — EXPERIMENTAL

Nambu Experimental shown disassembled. Many of the design features of pistols later produced by the Nambu Works can be seen here.

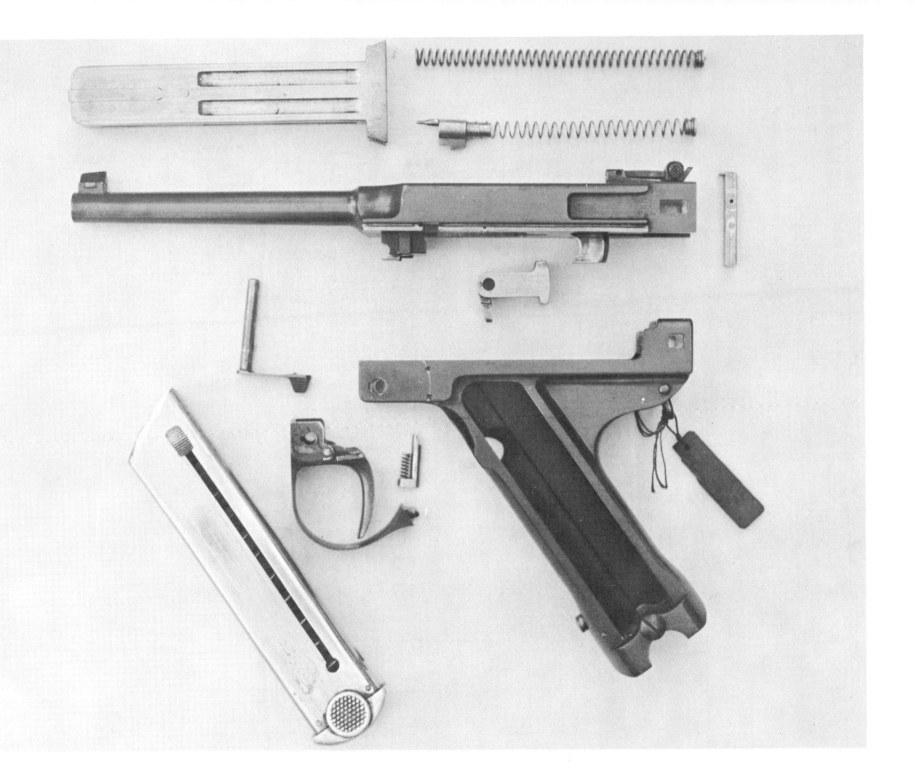

MODEL 14 (1925) PRESENTATION PIECE

This Pistol was evidently presented to an Air Force Officer by a Japanese Naval Base. The original finish has been re-blued. The Bronze Grips are both engraved as follows: "By Imperial Government to Air Force Captain Ieri — 1945 — Japanese Naval Base — Sasebo." The Pistol is a Nagoya October 1944 model.

Gary Cufley Collection

Typical installation of lanyard loop on early small trigger guard model.

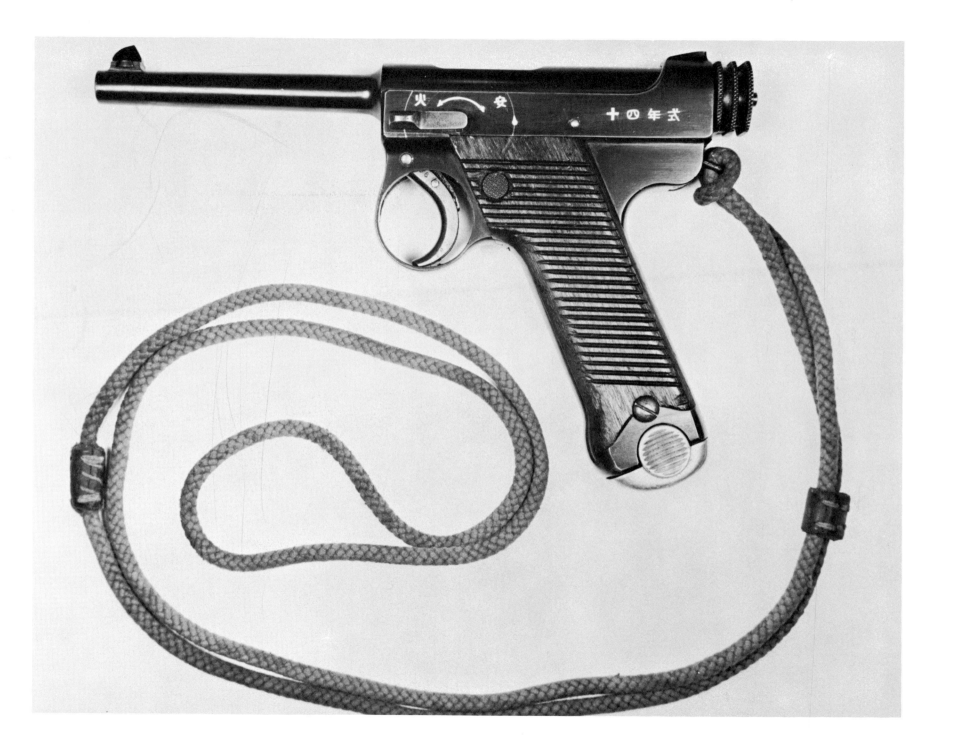

A reprint of a page out of an early officer's training guide.
This shows the early type 1904 Nambu, holster, and all of its parts
properly labeled in Japanese.

第九図　陸式拳銃ノ各部及附属品ノ名称

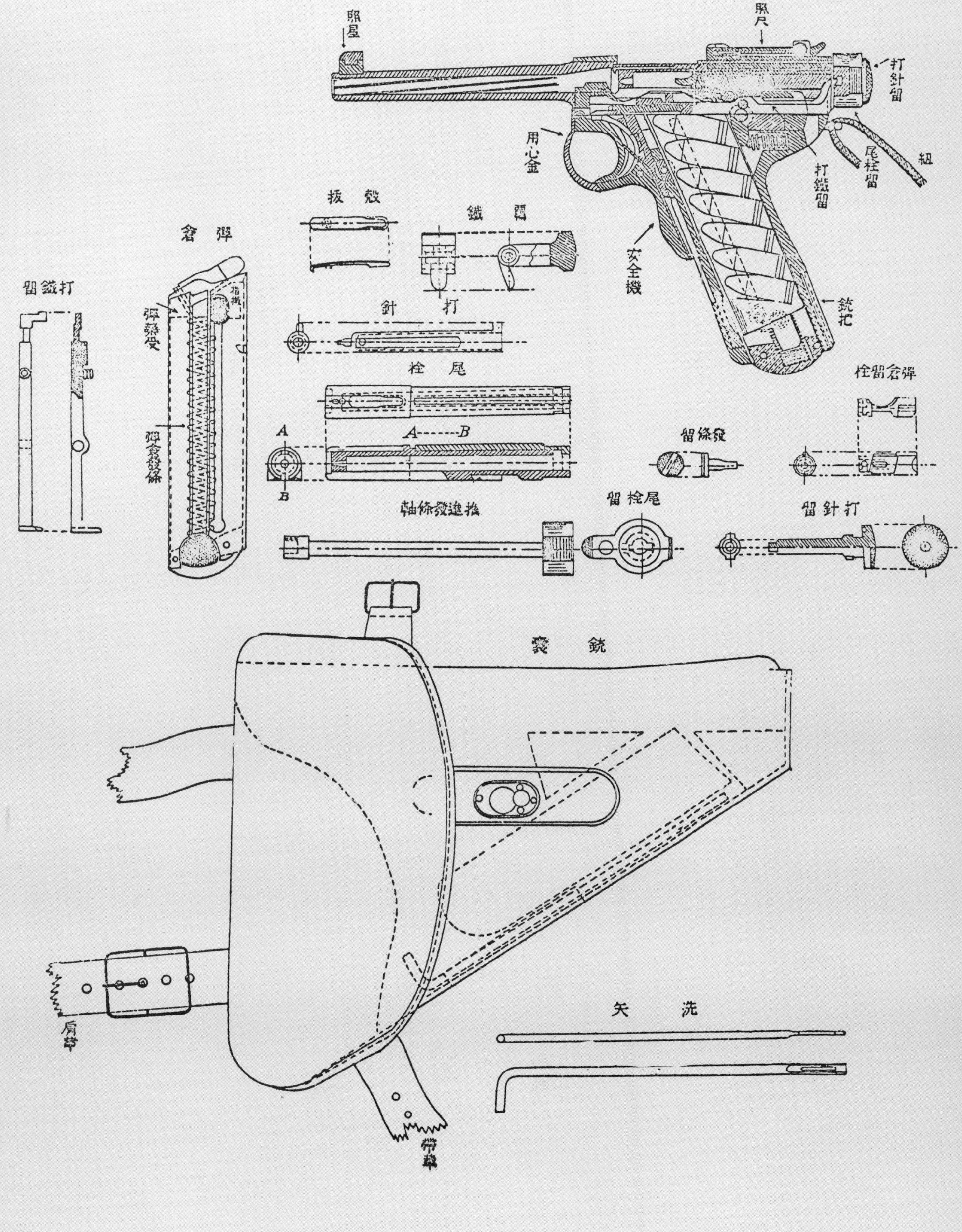

NATIONAL DEFENSE PISTOL

As it became more obvious that Japan was losing the war, the Military decided invasion of the Homeland was inevitable. This pistol was to make that invasion as costly as possible to the Allies. It is a single-shot, black powder cap and ball of approximately 11mm. Plans for construction from the most basic materials (pipe, strap iron, tin sheet) were distributed to the civilian population. The idea was for as many civilians as possible to each have one shot at the invasion troops. Multiplying this by the population of Japan at that time gives quite an impressive amount of firepower.

Courtesy of P. J. Piene

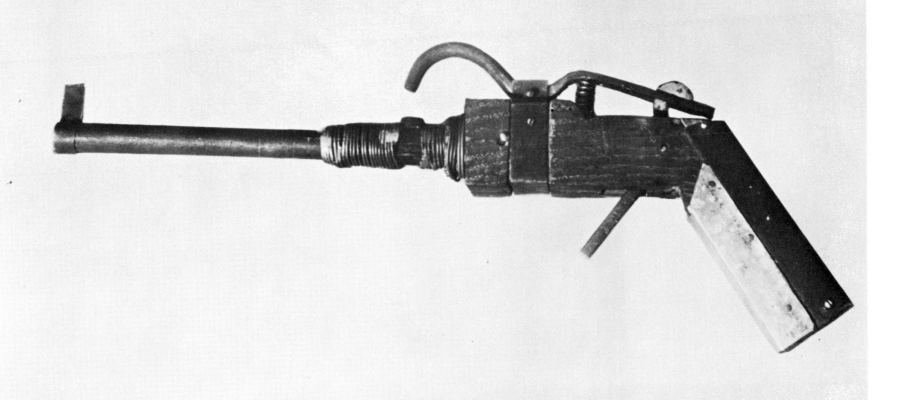